# The Effective Use
# of Market Research

# The Effective Use of MARKET RESEARCH

## A Guide for Management

Revised and Updated Edition

## Robin Birn

KOGAN
PAGE

To Danit and Daniel

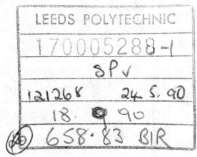
© Robin J. Birn 1988, 1990

First published in 1988 by
Kogan Page Ltd
120 Pentonville Road
London N1 9JN

Revised edition, 1990

Printed and bound in Great Britain by
Richard Clay Ltd, Bungay, Suffolk
Typeset by DP Photosetting, Aylesbury, Bucks

*British Library Cataloguing in Publication Data*
Birn, Robin J.
    The effective use of market research. — Rev. ed.
    1. Market research.
    I. Title.
    658.8'3

ISBN 0-7494-0149-4

# Contents

# Foreword

Market researchers have a unique role to play in guiding others through the necessary changes in business life. Their training and background should provide an 'additive element' to any situation in which they get involved. They need to be analytical, questioning, objective, stimulating, and to fulfil a role which gives a maximum 'value added' service.

Marketing is a relatively young business discipline which is constantly changing and growing as its techniques become more widely used and accepted. Most of the disciplines of the marketing mix are 'common sense' and their application is the focal point of any business activity.

Market research is sometimes seen, even today, merely as information gathering. In fact, when properly structured, it can make a valuable contribution to a company's understanding of its products, its markets, and its overall business strategy.

## The aim of the book

The aim of this book is to review how the application of market research techniques can improve marketing decisions. The views expressed have developed through the experience of working with companies with diverse marketing problems.

All research applications can be classified into four types: market analysis, product performance analysis, marketing performance analysis, and communications performance analysis. This book investigates the use of each of these applications and, through case studies, describes the actions some companies were able to take as a result of completing marketing projects.

It does not claim to lay down definitive rules for the application of research to decision making. It presents a series of examples for the marketing manager or researcher to consider in relation to his own company, product, service, market and customers. These examples show that users of market research are widening their implementation of the techniques, and applying them to help their companies take effective decisions.

The aim is not to show the reader how to carry out market research by reviewing the technicalities involved: these can be sourced by referring to the recommended booklist at the end of the book. This book is an aid for those who are not familiar with research but who want to incorporate the research findings into management and marketing decision-making. Specifically, it discusses:

- the management and marketing situations in which market research is required by a company
- the decision-making process for using research in particular marketing situations
- the effect of using research to assist companies in deciding on the marketing and sales actions they can take, if the findings of the research are implemented effectively.

# Acknowledgements

This book could not have been written without the help of everyone I have worked with, whether within a company or in the client versus marketing services role. I am therefore grateful to all of them; when they read the book they may well recognize ideas derived from conversations that we have had in the past.

Special thanks are due to a number of people in the preparation of this book:

My wife, Danit, was partly responsible for this book reaching the publisher. Without her support I would not have found time to write it. Her hard work at the word processor made sure that we did not over-run the deadline.

Brian Dickson, Sales & Marketing Director, Scobie & McIntosh Ltd, Edinburgh, has been of enormous help through the many discussions and planning sessions, and the support he has provided over the years as both client and colleague. I am particularly grateful to him for preparing Chapter 11, 'The Effective Use of Market Research'. Based on some ideas we developed for a paper called 'It's not the research, it's the action after the research' presented at the Annual Market Research Society Conference a few years ago, it provides an insight into the 'research user's' point of view. The application of research to decision-making, marketing and sales planning often fails to live up to its potential because of insufficient development of the research structure and the requirement for careful questionnaire design. This chapter demonstrates the benefits of structured research.

**11**

Thanks are also due to the following people:
Derrick Mitchell, Sales and Marketing Director, Devro Ltd, Glasgow, for providing the details on his company and how it has used research. Mike Chittleburgh of John Bartholomew & Son Ltd, and Peter Mouncey, Lindsey Edwards and Brian Stelling of the Automobile Association, founder members of the UK Map, Atlas and Guide Book research, for allowing me to publish some of the research findings. Pauline Geake, Director of Research and Auditing Services Ltd, for assisting me in the fieldwork for some of the projects discussed in the book. Phyllis Vangelder, editor of *Survey* and the *Market Research Society Newsletter*, for her support. This was appreciated both in the early days of planning the book in pushing me to develop the concepts, and for her expert advice in selecting suitable case studies for inclusion in the book. The writers of the case studies selected from *Survey*. Without the work the points made in this book would not be as well illustrated as they are. Sandy Ewert, Scottish Development Agency, and Sultan Kermally, Management Centre Europe (American Management Association), as without their requests for support, I would not have had material to develop into the chapters of this book.

Chapter 9 was first published in a shortened format in 1988 in *The Sales Management Handbook*, edited by Patrick Forsyth of Marketing Improvements Ltd. I am grateful to both him and Gower Publishing for allowing me to use that chapter as the basis for my theme 'Assessing and Improving the Sales Process'.

Lastly, thanks are due to Kogan Page, for including the book in their Professional Paperback series.

# 1

# The Increasing Use of Market Research

**The growth of the market for market research**

How often has a marketing manager been heard to ask, 'Why do I need market research? I know what my customers want and I know that my products are the best and I expect that our new products will sell well. In our experience there are still some people in industry even today who hold this negative attitude towards market research.

However, market research has been gaining momentum in the past few years, and the recent rapid growth of the industry is an indication of the extent to which management has been persuaded to take it seriously.

Traditionally, though, marketing management in most sectors of industry, whether consumer, industrial, retail or services, has concentrated marketing on protecting their *existing* products, and nurturing them to become healthier and more profitable. These companies have used the techniques of market research to help develop and market their products at the level of customer acceptance most effective and profitable for them in terms of the business objectives already decided on.

Over the last 15 years the use of market research has broadened, and marketing management in some companies is looking to less traditional styles of marketing. They have taken on different types of market research activities to help them find their way to new markets, new products and new customers. Various examples can be cited: companies who have been dissatisfied with their current sales, current markets, and thus their overall marketing performance, have used research to find out how their sales and market performance can be improved; companies who have wanted to find out a lot more about their markets, thus enabling them to optimize their sales and marketing activities, have done this by commissioning research to find out how to evaluate their relationships with their distributors, or their wholesalers, or their agents; companies seeking new opportunities by looking at new markets with existing products, or new markets with new products, have done this by commissioning the traditional new product development research programmes.

The trend that has emerged as a result of these different types of applications of market research is an increase in market research activity, designed to give marketing management guidance as to what marketing actions they should be adopting for the future.

The worldwide market for commercial market research is now worth about £2,400 million, of which the US accounts for about 45 per cent, the UK 9 per cent, and the rest of Europe another 26 per cent. A recent analysis shows that total expenditure on market research worldwide nearly doubled in six years.

Since 1983 the expenditure in the UK has grown considerably, resulting in the UK becoming the biggest West European market research market. A survey of research suppliers completed at the end of 1987 by the Technical and Development Committee of the Market Research Society showed that the UK market research industry was worth £222 million in 1986. This industry total does not cover research conducted directly by manufacturers and service companies, nor that carried out by organizations not listed in the *Market Research Yearbook*. The distribution of the turnover of the industry is shown in Table 1.1 from which it can be seen that by far the greatest expenditure is in the consumer markets.

The market research industry undertakes 17.5 million interviews per year, of which 8 million involve face-to-face contact. Postal/self-completion and telephone surveys each account for approximately 4.5 million interviews (see Table 1.2).

The market for quantitative research – research which seeks to measure markets – is dominated by quantitative surveys which account for 81 per cent of turnover. Qualitative research – involving group

**Table 1.1** Turnover of the market research industry by market category (1986)

|  | £m | % |
| --- | --- | --- |
| Consumer | **169.6** | **76** |
| Retail/wholesale | 19.4 | 9 |
| Business/industrial | 20.4 | 9 |
| Medical | 9.7 | 4 |
| Agricultural | 3.0 | 1 |
| **Total** | **222.1** |  |

(*Source:* Market Research Society)

**Table 1.2** Distribution by category of market research interviews conducted in the UK (1986 figures)

| Interviews Conducted | No. (million) | % Value | % Volume |
| --- | --- | --- | --- |
| **Face-to-face** | **8.2** | **47** | **85** |
| Hall tests | 0.7 | 4 | 8 |
| Group discussions | 0.3 | 2 | 12 |
| Other personal | 7.2 | 41 | 65 |
| **Postal/self-completion** | 4.7 | 27 | 5 |
| **Telephone** | 4.6 | 26 | 10 |
| **Total** | **17.5** |  |  |

(*Source:* Market Research Society)

discussions or in-depth interviews, with findings based on content – accounts for £32 million turnover and is largely concentrated on product and advertising development.

The activities of the whole industry are mainly concerned with improving manufacturers' and service providers' understanding of customer needs, their motivations and opinions, rather than merely measuring existing behaviour (see Table 1.3). Thus research is playing an important part in helping companies know what the market wants

**Table 1.3** Category of consumer research

| | Total £170m | | Quantitative £138m | | Qualitative £32m | |
|---|---|---|---|---|---|---|
| | £m | % | £m | % | £m | % |
| Product development | 35 | 21 | 25 | 18 | 10 | 31 |
| Advertising, testing, and development | 38 | 22 | 28 | 20 | 10 | 31 |
| Product usage, satisfaction, attitude and usage studies | 40 | 24 | 31 | 22 | 9 | 28 |
| Market measurement | 46 | 27 | 46 | 33 | * | * |
| Social and opinion studies | 11 | 6 | 8 | 6 | 3 | 9 |

(*Source:* Market Research Society)

and manage the changes in their marketing, sales and communication methods.

The most interesting development in recent years is that market research is no longer the preserve of the fast-moving consumer goods companies on which the industry was founded. These companies now account for only 38 per cent of the total activity, the remainder being spread across a wide range of industries (see Table 1.4).

During 1986 the market research industry made a contribution to the UK trade balance of more than £8 million. In fact, since the last recession, marketing management has looked increasingly to market research to aid in decision-making. More and more companies are appreciating the importance of strategic decisions, placing more emphasis on these than on tactical decisions.

**Case studies**

Here are two examples of how research assisted companies' activities. In a conscious effort to spend their budgets carefully two companies collected information through desk research on both their products and their markets.

**Table 1.4** Expenditure of companies commissioning research

| Type of commissioning company | £m | % |
|---|---|---|
| Consumer goods | 85 | 38 |
|     Food/soft drinks | 40 | 18 |
|     Health/beauty aids | 14 | 6 |
|     Alcohol/tobacco | 16 | 7 |
|     Household/hardware | 15 | 7 |
| Advertising agencies | 16 | 7 |
| Press/TV | 15 | 7 |
| Public services | 15 | 7 |
| Banking/insurance | 14 | 6 |
| Industrial products | 13 | 6 |
| Pharmaceutical | 12 | 5 |
| Vehicles/oil companies | 12 | 5 |
| Central & local government | 9 | 4 |
| Travel/tourism | 8 | 4 |
| Retailers | 8 | 4 |
| Other | 15 | 7 |
| **Total** | **222** | |

(*Source:* Market Research Society)

A manufacturer of waste disposal products researched the market for new product opportunities through basic desk research. The company analysed the data and used it to take a decision to develop a prototype for a new product, which the company believed could fill a market gap.

Another manufacturer of garden products collected information on its markets by carrying out basic desk research and by talking to 'market experts' in independent research houses and advisory bodies, and executives from gardening and leisure journals. As a result, the company was able to take the decision to invest in new tooling for the development of a new product.

This research was therefore a very cost-effective way of taking important marketing decisions, and it also led them to design research projects which analysed further the product opportunities in their markets.

The manufacturer of waste disposal products decided to research the

needs of its distributors and then the needs of the end-users. This style of project provided the company with information on its markets and on where the company stood with its distributors in relation to its competitors. In addition, it helped provide the company with information on how the target markets perceived the company and how its competitors were failing to capitalize on the market opportunities.
 , The result of carrying out such research was as follows:

- the manufacturer of the waste disposal product was able to design a more practical product than any currently on the market. They were then able to successfully market the product through the distributors, having analysed and taken into account their needs.
- the manufacturer of the garden products decided on a product design which the company believed would fill the gap in the market that it had identified through its research.

Both of these companies then organized a new product development programme based on research amongst their target markets for their products. Their research was specifically designed to provide information which could lead them to take marketing actions. It therefore helped them to get where they wanted to go in their respective markets, by providing actionable information.

The key benefit derived from this type of research by both companies was that analysis of the market helped them analyse the productivity of their marketing activities. Both companies therefore:

- analysed the productivity of their marketing methods, by measuring their effectiveness and acceptability to both distributors and customers.
- researched the needs of the distribution channels to help bring about relevant marketing decisions and implement marketing methods which were more appropriate for the company's current markets and products.
- obtained data on their marketing activities and that of their competitors as perceived by their distributors and customers.

This helped both companies strengthen and improve their business and increase market share.

Normally, market research techniques are divided into the following different types:

- desk research
- consumer research
- product research
- advertising research
- retail research
- industrial research
- agricultural research
- social research and opinion research.

None of these types of research techniques in their true sense was used individually to solve the marketing problems of either the manufacturer of the waste disposal product or the manufacturer of the garden product. In fact, they used a combination of them, which enabled the companies to make effective decisions, because the application of these techniques had to be made in relation to financial considerations. Large-scale survey research would have provided the information they required, but the cost would have been prohibitive to both of these companies.

The application of research techniques to marketing decision-making is likely to be the reason for the continuing growth of the use of market research services in the future. Some companies already apply the techniques effectively but others are still learning how to use them.

The benefit of applying research techniques in the way illustrated above is that marketing decisions can be implemented in the most cost-effective way.

In the UK it has become more widely accepted that sustained growth in business, profit and jobs can only come from improved performance in the marketplace and an increased share of world trade, in both export and import substitution. As a result, the Government is actively persuading companies to allow management to go through formal evaluation of their sales and marketing methods. Through the Department of Trade and Industry Enterprise Initiative, the Government is helping small and medium-sized companies to improve their marketing effectiveness and performance to the level achieved in most successful UK and international businesses. This and other schemes such as the Scottish Development Agency Scheme for small businesses, the Better Business Services Scheme and the British Overseas Trade Board Export Market Research Scheme, are all available to provide companies with financial support to develop their marketing and research activities.

**19**

# 2

# Decision Making and the Need for Research

Decision making is central to carrying out all managerial functions to make the planning and monitoring process work. Good decisions are taken on the basis of availability and use of relevant information. The information of most concern to marketing management comes from markets and customers, present, potential and future, and concerns the shape, size, nature, needs, opportunities and threats within the market. Market research is the means of providing them with that information.

## Definition of market research

The traditional definition of market research is:

'The systematic problem analysis, model-building and fact-finding for the purpose of improved decision-making and control in the marketing of goods and services.'

This implies that research is not just an information tool but a means of providing guidance to help improve the abilities of management within an organization, as well as a means of making a contribution to the management of the marketing mix. It can be used to help decide on: the marketing strategy required to meet the challenge of new opportunities; which market gaps to approach; and which are the key areas of interest for future marketing strategies.

## Purposes of market research

The two basic purposes of research are:

- to reduce uncertainty when plans are being made, whether these relate to the marketing operation as a whole or to individual components of the marketing mix such as advertising or sales promotion.
- to monitor performance after the plans have been put into operation. In fact, the monitoring role has two specific functions: it helps to control the execution of the company's operational plan and it makes a substantial contribution to long-term strategic planning.

## The role of marketing management

Management's aim is to satisfy its customers at a profit to the company. To achieve this it is necessary to keep up to date on a day-to-day basis with the complex and changing marketplace by commissioning research, visiting customers and distributors, discussing customer needs with the sales force, and, in some cases, sharing ideas with competitors through the auspices of an industrial or professional association.

The long-term management of the total business is more complex; it requires the setting of objectives and development of strategies. To achieve this it is important for management to set aside the day-to-day decision-making and take an overall look at the company, its operations and the allocation of resources for sales and marketing activities.

The setting of marketing objectives begins with a thorough analysis of the implications of the question, 'What business are we in?'. An attempt to analyse this question generates further questions, which help conceptualize the nature of the business activity and encourage an 'independent assessment' over and above the day-to-day tasks to see where the business is going.

These questions are:

1. *Where are we now?*
   This question can be answered by completing a marketing audit of the company's sales and marketing methods, which will in turn probably raise a number of other questions, highlight other problems

and establish where there is an information gap.

2. *Where do we want to go?*

This question can be answered by developing corporate marketing objectives, selecting corporate marketing strategies, and developing a marketing action plan to adopt a strategic approach to running the business. The answer to this question will provide a company with a structure within which to develop, run and monitor the sales and marketing methods required for managing the marketing mix.

3. *How will we get there?*

This question will be answered by considering the actions required by the whole company to implement the action plans. The answer will provide the company with the internal monitoring system it needs to run its operation.

## Marketing as a systematic process

Marketing is a systematic process which provides a technique for survival and growth. It requires creativity and innovation in order to:

- develop techniques to anticipate and identify customer needs, rather than wait for trends to become self-evident through the success of competitors.
- recognize that customers are often unaware of their 'unsatisfied' needs.
- develop and implement strategies and tactics for products, prices, promotion and distribution.
- develop and use techniques for evaluating the implemented strategies and tactics.

## Case study

Take, for example, the situation that the following company found itself in a few years ago.

Devro Ltd, established at Moodiesburn near Glasgow since 1964, employs some 600 people, producing casing from natural protein for a number of sausage manufacturers, including manufacturers for supermarket chains and high street butchers.

The company was not a newcomer to research: it was the search for new products by Devro's parent company, Johnson & Johnson, which led to the development of a process for manufacturing sausage casings from collagen – the most abundant, naturally occurring protein found in mammals.

Researchers have developed numerous products using the inherent strength and qualities of collagen. It is used in the manufacture of:

- wound and burn dressings
- cardiovascular applications in surgery
- microsurgery
- toiletries such as cosmetics and shampoo
- food and beverages, such as finings for wines, beer, fruit juices, confectionery products
- sausage casings.

Discovering that collagen from cattle hides could be extruded into a tube with uniformly thin walls, Devro (Development and Research Organisation) realized the importance of these implications for the sausage manufacturer. Consequently, Johnson & Johnson created a worldwide organization with Devro companies in the US, Australia, Canada and the UK, the latter being Devro Ltd. This resulted in the creation of a range of products which sausage manufacturers, on an international scale, have proved give real productivity benefits in the manufacture of fresh and smoked sausage.

The retail sausage market in the UK is a £550 million market representing 290,000 tonnes of sausages annually (equivalent to two sausages per person every week). From 1972 to 1982 the market showed little or no change, varying by less than 7 per cent over the period. This static situation was a result of, on the one hand, the decline in the number of people and families eating a cooked breakfast, due to a change in lifestyles and to the heavy marketing and advertising activity of the breakfast cereal companies; and, on the other:

- the switching of sausage consumption from breakfast to other meal times, particularly snacks eaten both in and out of the home.
- the move to eating sausages rather than other more expensive meat because of the need for households to run balanced budgets during tight economic conditions.
- the growth of 'convenience foods' and the resulting switch of eating

habits to other inexpensive foods.
- the marketing activities of the sausage manufacturers which concentrate on brand share growth rather than the expansion of the total market.

The sausage market presented itself as a market in possible incipient decline, with new ideas and new marketing activities only affecting brand share of individual producers or supermarket own-label products, rather than the total market.

Within this context, the sausage casing market was worth over £40 million, representing 1 million kilometres of casing. It reflected the state of the retail sausage market, as the total casing market had shown the same relative static position over the period 1972–1982.

Devro Ltd, however, competing with a supplier using animal gut, three other collagen casing suppliers and a supplier of cellulose casing for skinless sausage, had grown continuously over this ten-year period. Its growth was attributable to having a good product sold at the right price, giving its buyers high productivity gains in the manufacture of sausages, and the fact that it is a technically superior product to animal gut – the original source of casing. Devro Ltd had entered and served the sausage casing market through an aggressive and effective selling operation which had helped to increase its market share year by year, at the expense of other collagen casing manufacturers, while replacing the use of animal gut.

From 1974 to 1979, sales had grown by over 200 per cent, but in 1980 sales during the beginning of the year suddenly fell in comparison with the previous year's sales. As a result, the company questioned once again in detail the basic and original marketing questions necessary for all sales and marketing operations:

- What is happening in the sausage and sausage casing markets?
- Is it only Devro Ltd's sales that have dropped, or is it a result of a market decline?
- What could the company's competitors be doing differently that may affect Devro Ltd's sales?
- What marketing strategies do we need to adopt to recover lost sales or create new ones?

25

- What can Devro Ltd, as an industrial marketing company supplying sausage casings, do in order to influence our customer's market and therefore influence the casing market?

Devro Ltd had to concentrate on quantifying and evaluating the fundamental questions:

1. Where is our market now?
2. Where is it going?
3. How do we get where it is going?

as well as assessing

4. What are the trends in our customers' markets?
5. How is the market influenced?
6. How can we expand the market?

For the first three questions to be answered, the market had to be evaluated and existing activities reappraised by asking further questions, ie:

1. *Where is our market now?*
   - Is the market changing in size, structure, location or nature?
   - Are there gaps in the market to be exploited?
   - What are our competitors doing in comparison with us?
   - Who are our potential competitors?
   - What is the 'market map' of this market?
   - What is our market segmentation?
   - Do we understand the needs of our customers and their customers?
   - Do we have sufficient qualitative and quantitative research data?
   - What are our marketing activities to meet the needs of this market?
   - What sales strategy should we adopt?
   - What PR, advertising and promotional activities should we be considering?
2. *Where do we want to go?*
   - What are the corporate marketing objectives we need?
   - What are our corporate marketing strategies?
   - Have the four major categories of strategy – market penetration, market development, product development and diversification – been investigated?

3. *How will we get there?*
   - What are our approaches to marketing planning?
   - What marketing staff do we need to implement this plan?
   - What staffing do we need?
   - How do the staff develop their knowledge and skills?
   - What do we need to do to evaluate and control our marketing activity?

The first decision that faced the company was to agree what type of research activity it needed to carry out. The research could include:

- identifying the acceptability of sausage casings
- researching the needs of supermarket chains and butchers, because they are the key influencers of the sale of the final product
- identifying what key promotional activity, concentrated sales activity and market positioning would be needed to recover lost sales.

However, this type of research programme would only assist the company in the short term. What was really required was a research programme for the long term which would answer the first three key questions by examining:

- how to establish and develop the casing market or, alternatively, the sausage market for both Devro Ltd's and its customers' benefit.
- what new products would be required to assist market development in both markets.
- what marketing strategies and actions would be required to sustain such growth and secure the customer base.

We will see later in this book what research solution Devro Ltd selected to answer the key questions.

## Collecting research data

Any information that is collected in market research is basically concerned with two things:

1. *What is happening in the market?* (classified as *performance* data).
2. *Why is it happening?* (classified as *behaviour* and *attitude* data).

*Performance data*

Performance data may well be data that is available to the company at present, but which has probably not been collected formally or with any meaningful objective market analysis. It would include:

- consumer sales, both the company's and its competitors'
- trade purchases and stock levels
- distribution levels achieved
- the effectiveness of marketing communication, such as consumer advertising recall and understanding, and the number of enquiries resulting from an advertisement
- the performance of products in use
- the levels of trade support achieved, such as point of sales displays.

*Behaviour data*

Behaviour data is more likely to be information that has to be collected externally about the market and its needs. This includes information concerning:

- who is purchasing or not purchasing – consumers and their characteristics, demographics and life styles
- what goods, sizes, styles and colours are bought
- where the products are bought
- how often they are bought
- for what main purpose and use they are bought
- what are the shopping habits, use of leisure time, general spending habits, life style, TV watching, radio listening, and newspapers, journals, trade journal reading habits, etc.

*Attitude research*

Attitude data can be derived from a homogeneous group of customers, or individual groups of product/service users, by monitoring:

- their perceived need for the products or services
- their evaluation of products or services used or not used
- how they view the attributes of specific products or services
- their buying criteria for the products or services
- different ways of satisfying their needs
- the price at which the product or service is acceptable

- their reactions to aspects of company presentations and communications, and the sources of supply and distribution channels
- their assessment of other people and their life styles.

In the marketing of goods or services the above categories of data are of use throughout the marketing planning process, from identifying new or changed customer needs and wants, to identifying feasible objectives and strategies, to evaluating the effectiveness of the various tactics used, to identifying the effectiveness of competitor activity and its results.

## A structured approach to decision making

Decision-making in marketing is similar to that in any other managerial function. It depends on establishing:

1. Where or why an action or decision should be taken.
2. What action or decision is indicated.
3. What is the result of implementing the action or decision and what are the implications for future actions or decisions.

A continuous flow of marketing research information is therefore needed to manage the process of decision-making. Figure 2.1 shows how the appropriate research information is supplied at each stage in the decision-making process.

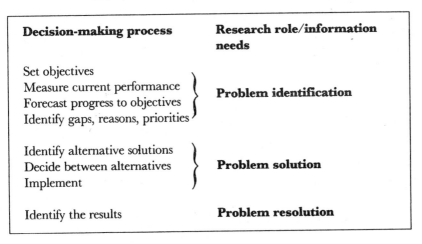

Figure 2.1 Research for decision making

The quality of the information gained from marketing research and its contribution to decision-making to a large extent depend on the definition of the problem. Without a clear definition of the problem research becomes an isolated piece of information. This information might be interesting but it would not necessarily provide management with the means of refining their decisions; the research would fail to provide the 'lead' towards the sales and marketing actions that are required. Any approach to designing a research project must therefore start with problem definition. After this, careful discussion on the type of research that is required and what should be gained from it is essential if a company is to make an investment in effective and cost-effective market research. Marketing management will ask the following types of questions to help to decide what research to carry out to solve the problem:

- What information will help us make our decisions?
- What are we going to do with this information?
- How should we collect this information?
- What are we going to measure?
- How should we analyse the results?
- How much should we spend on collecting the information?

It is important to consider too the 'cost and value' of information that may be obtained. However, this in itself is meaningless unless management clearly identifies the benefits of using the research. To do this, they need to weigh up the likely outcome of not using research against the likely results of using it. They therefore need to ask the following questions:

- What decision am I faced with?
- What is the potential cost of taking the wrong decision?
- What is the probability or risk of taking a wrong decision on the basis of information already available?
- How justified am I in taking this decision without collecting new data?
- How will additional information help me?
- How quickly is any additional information required?
- What level of accuracy is required?

By answering these questions, marketing management can identify a set of 'action standards' with which they must comply for the company to function successfully. The most appropriate and cost-effective research necessary to help them meet these standards can then be ascertained.

The process outlined in Fig. 2.1 will help the marketing manager think through the problem, define it, assess what alternative courses of action or decisions will follow from the range of information that *could* be acquired and, finally, decide what *must* be acquired to be 'safe' – ie what action standards he must work to. The essential thing is to determine in advance the most likely alternatives or hypotheses and use these to identify the 'action standards'.

Figure 2.2 shows the steps involved in designing an effective research project, and the questions to consider at each stage.

| STEP | QUESTIONS TO CONSIDER |
|---|---|
| Problem definition | What decision and type of information will help? |
| Decide the value of information | What is the cost/risk/loss of opportunity in taking the wrong decisions? |
| Select data collection methods | What secondary, survey and experimentation methods and variations are needed? |
| Select measurement techniques | Which questionnaires, attitude scales, observation and/or projective techniques are required? |
| Select the sample | Which and how many respondents or things should be measured? |
| Select the analytical method | Depends on the sample and the questionnaire |
| Specify the time and the cost | Depends on the value of the information |
| Prepare the research proposal | |
| Evaluate and implement the proposal | |

**Figure 2.2** Designing the research project

Effective research, therefore, depends on the management team formally adopting this structured approach to decision making. This means deciding in advance what is required from the research rather than finding out facts and making an interpretation which merely relies on 'a professional judgement'. The planning in itself helps to define the problem and refine the extent to which information needs to be collected. It also influences the way in which a research project is designed: it not only shows management who needs to be interviewed, but also helps to shape the nature of the questioning for the question-naire. The development of the right questions therefore can be concentrated on proving or disproving a hypothesis of a marketing, product or communications concept. In doing so it also helps to think through the options that management can consider once the research has been completed.

### Guidelines for decision-making

- Remember that research is only of use if it *serves an end to a purpose and is acted on*.
- Think not only about your own market but the market of your competitors and your customers.
- Measure the total consumption or the use of your product and your competitors' products.
- Work out who the ultimate consumer is and what he or she requires of your product.
- Plan to develop your products or related products.
- Do not be complacent, even if your product is selling well at present. Research your market to anticipate market needs.

### Checklist of questions on the use of research

- How can research reduce the uncertainty of sales or marketing planning?
- Will market research help the company to improve the marketing and sales decision-making process?
- What information do we need to assist in the decision-making process?

- Have we research information which provides sufficient data on:
  **market analysis** – do we know the 'geography' of the market?
  **product performance analysis** – do our products meet the standards of consumer acceptance set for them?
  **marketing performance analysis** – are we using the most effective sales and marketing methods to meet our customer needs and counter competitors' methods?
  **communications performance analysis** – have we changed the attitudes of our customers through our advertising and promotions? Do our customers understand our advertising and promotions?
- Do we see ourselves as our customers see us?
- Are our systems and total attitude to our sales and marketing geared to 'thinking of the customer'?
- Are we communicating all of the benefits of our products to our customers?
- Where is our market now?
- Where do we want to go?
- How will we get there?
- Have we identified the research problem?
- What is the best research solution?
- What do we need to monitor once we have put our marketing, sales and advertising plans into action?

# 3

# Analysing Markets

**The need for objective external research**

Most companies collect information on their markets in order to monitor the success of their business. Indeed, some research their markets to check that there is business in existence for them to survive in the future.

Many companies take the view that as they are already doing market research, they do not need the services of independent marketing and research companies; computer data on customers and information from distributors, as well as feedback about customers' needs from their own salesmen, all seem sufficient market information.

Whereas this type of information is essential for the day-to-day management of a company, it is not necessarily the right information on which to base important decisions relating to marketing strategies. In addition, most of this information is historical and cannot project future trends in markets.

Research in industry has shown that unless a company is in a mass consumer market, it is likely that its marketing management lack the data essential for determining the future of its marketing. There will of course be exceptions, but experience of a number of assignments with clients has shown that companies are basically all seeking answers to the same key questions about their markets, which include assessing what is happening in their markets and identifying what their market share is. (The full list of these questions is given in the checklist on pp 46–8.) To

**35**

do this successfully, marketing management needs to use external research facilities to provide market analysis, the purpose of which is to measure and describe the 'geography' of the market. This new picture can then be compared with the introspective viewpoint and marketing decisions taken in the light of this comparison.

Despite resistance to external analysis from British industry up until the 1970s, in recent years management in both manufacturing and service companies have realized the benefits of an independent, objective viewpoint, and are using external market research companies far more readily.

## The market analysis

Market analysis is used to:

- identify the overall trends of sales in a market.
- identify likely changes in the short and long term.
- use these trends to forecast as accurately as possible the future activities in the market, taking into account the trends and their effects.
- determine whether the market in terms of its size is suitable for the company to enter, remain in or expand.

## Creating a market 'map'

The best way of answering the key questions for market analysis is to map out all of the features of the market in which a company is operating in terms of its size, shape and overall nature. This method will assist marketing management to get to know the structure of a market.

The key questions that need to be answered for compiling this map are:

- How do we define our markets?
- What is the size of our markets?
- What is the nature of these markets?
- Who are the companies in these markets?
- What is the nature of the companies' products or services and overall marketing activities?
- What are the products made of?

**36**

- Which distribution channels are used for each market?
- What other marketing methods are used?

Once these questions have been answered, a company then has sufficient information to look at a market in detail and decide on its marketing strategy. The real benefit is derived from taking the information gathered from compilation of internal records, experience of the company and external research, and plotting it on a 'market map' (an example of which is shown in Fig 3.1). In this way the mechanisms of the market can be seen clearly and the various elements of the market can then be quantified. Doing this on a regular basis can help to identify trends more easily and predict future changes more accurately.

The preparation of the market map depends on the use of a series of different research techniques. The suitability of each technique and its use depends on the advice and guidance a company receives from individual research consultancies, in relation to specific marketing problems. The following are examples of situations in which the company commissioned market analysis and was helped by the provision of a market map:

- A well known and successful occupational health products company which lacked market data needed to define the size of its own market. The result of mapping its market was to help define the opportunities for future growth outside its own sector. (See Fig 3.1.)
- A meat products company needed to undertake new product development. Prior to this it had to define the size of the new market and estimate the potential for the new product. Mapping the market clarified the extent of the product development opportunity.
- A clothing company which had no formal marketing development strategy and which was 'production led' was finding market growth difficult to obtain. Research in the market allowed the company to map the key opportunities in the marketplace, and determine the required level of penetration in the market, purchase frequencies and consumer profiles.

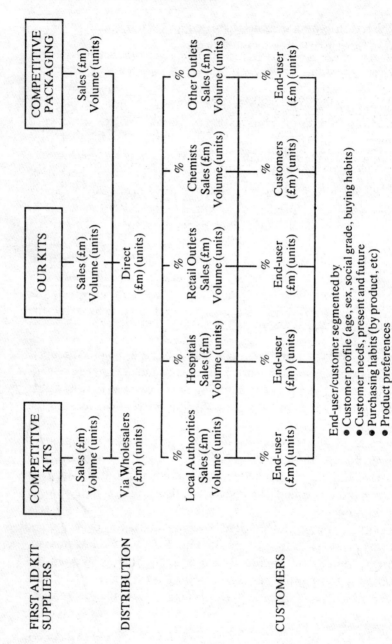

**Figure 3.1** Example of a market map – occupational health sector

### Guidelines for commissioning external research

Whichever situation a company finds itself in, there are certain common points to bear in mind when commissioning research.

1. Market analysis can be completed by answering the questions given in the checklist (pp 46–8), but the success of the analysis depends on the type of market being analysed. For example, a consumer market is easier to analyse than an industrial market. This is mainly because consumer markets are better researched and documented by the government and independent research organizations. Also, there is more data available in libraries and from other sources of information. Indeed, industrial markets sometimes have to be analysed by taking the limited published data available and then completing a mathematical analysis of 'known relationships' in terms of the actual sales of products or purchases made by customers. These reasoned 'guesstimates' are acceptable within certain marketing situations and limits.

2. The market analysis should not be completed solely through desk research and simply by searching through existing sources of information. Telephone interviews and, preferably, personal interviews are also effective. Members of a trade association or an executive in a government department responsible for the legislation affecting a particular industry are useful people to contact. Other market experts such as journalists and consultants are valuable sources of information in an initial market analysis. This is because their opinions add qualitative information on the trends within a market or product sector and the underlying reasons behind these trends. These people have regular contact with the key management and marketing personnel within manufacturing or service companies in the sectors on which they concentrate. They therefore have a good idea of what is happening in the sector and thus can even provide a 'guesstimate' on facts such as the size of the market and details of successful products and companies.

3. When market analysis is undertaken it is essential to be able to know, state and constantly refer to the sources of information used to compile the data. This is particularly important in relation to any data being used for sales forecasts, production forecasts, etc, as these

need to be accurate in order to predict the current and future market situation.

## Using market research

Marketing management needs to agree that an external market analysis is necessary for taking marketing decisions. External analysis is appropriate in certain specific situations:

- Where company personnel may have pre-conceived attitudes about a market, product field or perceived business opportunity, an independent viewpoint is helpful.
- Where the marketing problem or opportunity has a degree of sensitivity which requires a market analysis to be completed with total anonymity, or where there is a need for security, an independent organization can be used to screen the identity of an interested party.

More generally:

- Existing resources in the marketing or research department may be supplemented through the use of an external company.
- Using an independent company provides an objective viewpoint provided that the company has knowledge of the industry, experience in researching the market and the ability to advise on the appropriate marketing actions.

Once the decision has been taken to commission the external market analysis, it is important for the marketing manager to inform the marketing and research company of:

- the market and marketing situation.
- the problems that need to be evaluated.
- the reasons why the problems have to be evaluated.
- the type of external support that is perceived to be beneficial to solve the marketing problems – pure research, research and consultancy, ad-hoc research, continuous research, etc.
- the degree to which the outside resource should be involved in the implementation of the initial work.

More detailed advice on briefing the research company is given in Chapter 11.

**40**

Once the market analysis is commissioned, marketing management should discuss the key questions given in the checklist, and agree them with the research company. The research company can then begin the market analysis by gathering all the necessary information.

## Sources of information

Government statistical publications:

- *Trade and Industry*
- *Business Monitors*
- *Monthly Digest of Statistics*
- *Social Trends*
- *Regional Trends*
- *Economic Trends*
- *British Business*
- *UK National Accounts*
- *UK Balance of Payments*
- *Economic Progress Report*
- *Report on the Census of Production*
- *Family Expenditure Survey*
- *Census of Distribution*
- *Overseas Trade Statistics.*

Reference to any of the above should assist in:

- assessing market shares and identifying the size and growth of existing and new markets
- determining the number of customers in a sector
- determining consumer expenditure in a sector
- identifying distribution channels
- determining pricing and price changes
- estimating world markets, assessing foreign competition in the UK and estimating shares of UK exports overseas.

Most of this information can be obtained from the Central Statistical Office or a large library, such as the Statistics and Market Intelligence Library. However, what is not well publicized is that the Department of Industry has individual sections looking after specific industry sectors, for example insurance and pension funds, chemicals, etc.

The National Economic Development Office (NEDO) publishes reports and videos covering: industrial performance, market prospects, trade, innovation, manpower, communications, macroeconomic details, finance, and energy. There are also the Economic Development Committees which publish reports based on an individual sector working group, eg Scotch whisky, construction, engineering, etc. Referral to the EDC secretariats also tends to yield useful market information and data and advice from experts who have an in-depth knowledge of a particular market.

*Business Libraries*
These are located at the central library in most cities and will ensure that they keep the most important reports published by the government. In addition, they usually keep:

- company reports and accounts of the top 1,000 companies
- company files containing press cuttings on these companies
- industry files containing press cuttings on industry sectors
- official statistics: UK government data, EEC, OECD and UN statistics
- directories, annual year books, standard industry lists and classifications, etc
- market reports; reports index and research index detailing published market research reports available for purchase.

*Commercial Sources of Information*
These include:

- The Financial Times Business Information Services
- The London Business School Information Service
- Extel
- Inter Company Comparisons
- Jordans Dataquest
- Frost & Sullivan Sector Reports
- GIRA Sector Reports
- Economist Intelligence Unit
- Mintel √
- Datastar
- MGN Marketing Manual.

*Trade Associations*

There are hundreds of associations that represent the interests of particular manufacturers or service providers. Some of these associations also have good library and information facilities. Their main contribution, however, is to be able to provide someone who can answer questions. Their staff have regular contact with the association members and thus have a wealth of market knowledge.

*Universities and Colleges*

Numerous research projects are completed by graduates and research graduates at universities, polytechnics and colleges. Some of the universities concentrate on various industries and thus have an intimate knowledge of various sectors, and some have departments for marketing their knowledge and research facilities, eg UNIVED at the University of Edinburgh, or the South Bank Polytechnic.

*Institutes and Professional Associations*

Organizations such as the Institute of Marketing and the Market Research Society hold information on industry sectors, markets, products, services, and on consultants and research organizations who can be contacted to obtain further information and help.

**Using the information**

Once this fairly exhaustive list of sources of information has been investigated, further research can be undertaken. Consulting senior officers of trade associations, individual consultants, specialist researchers, editors of trade journals, authors of specialist books and discussion papers, can yield additional useful information.

Detailed and full analysis of this data should then follow, particularly to allow the researcher to match the original list of questions with the information obtained. The data can then be applied to the market map, to fill in the gaps that exist in the analysis. In addition, as the main activities for this market analysis have been completed, the researcher would prepare a full report summarizing the details of the desk research.

The market map for the first aid sector on suppliers and distributors (Fig. 3.1) would have been prepared using the sequence of actions detailed in Fig. 3.2. Most of the information would have been prepared

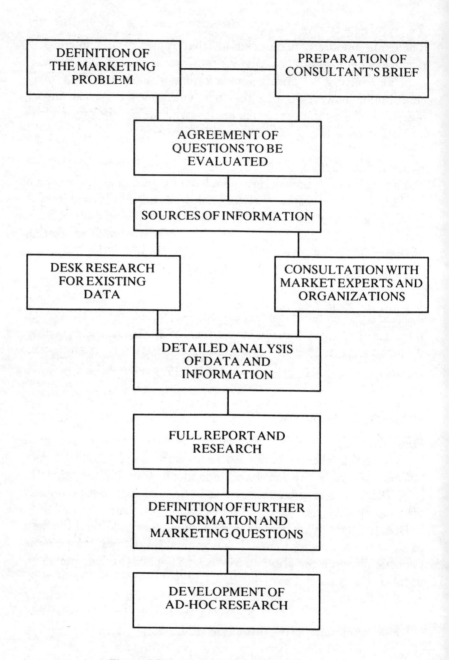

**Figure 3.2** Sequence for market analysis

from government sources, specialist sector research, referral to any published research, and discussions with market experts and consultants.

Very little market data and information is available on some markets because little work has been done by research companies and consultancies in providing useful data reports. In such cases it is possible for the marketing and research company to supplement the informal interviews with the market experts using scoping surveys. These scoping surveys are in-depth, detailed personal interviews with key management in selected companies in the sector.

Thus, by completing interviews with top managers of leading companies, a complete market overview can be prepared. This overview would be designed to answer the original questions set out for market analysis and to provide a total review of the market.

## Case study

Devro Ltd, the manufacturer of sausage casings described in Chapter 2, having defined what it wanted to do through the questioning process, decided its first step was to re-examine existing information sources on the casing and sausage markets. At that time this consisted of: detailed sales statistics and reports from salesmen, identifying customers' (sausage manufacturers') needs, and salesmen's reports on competitors activities; and quarterly reports from the National Food Survey (NFS), identifying consumer consumption patterns.

Since the size of the casing market was dependent on the size of the sausage market, in-depth analysis of the retail and catering sectors of the sausage market was undertaken.

For the retail sausage market, a predictive model of in-home consumption was formulated which gave a forward measurement of consumption by using continuous consumer panel data as a database. The panel data was used as an immediate record of consumption and then backed up by the use of NFS as confirmative data the following quarter.

In this way, an important step forward in using more immediately available panel data had been taken, rather than the traditional but 'historic' reporting of NFS. Equally important, this method of forecasting had not been used before in either the casing or sausage markets and its originality not only gave Devro Ltd a new planning tool, but also provided an information source for sausage manufacturers as well.

Once the retail sausage market had been defined, analysis of the catering market also brought new information to light. The industry had always understood the catering segment to be a fixed proportion of the retail sector – about 25–30 per cent. However, detailed analyses, through industry surveys and catering omnibus work, established that it was a sector in its own right and subject to different economic pressures.

This analysis allowed Devro Ltd not only to identify the size of the sausage market but also to confirm the size of the casing market. Devro Ltd could therefore monitor the movements in its markets, project future movements and predict the needs of the casing market in relation to the needs of the sausage market. In doing this, the company was able to provide its own production facilities with a longer-term look at the movements in the market than its salesmen had been able to provide.

It was realized that although the reports then available provided some information on market trends, they gave only part of the picture. The ability to answer the key marketing questions required more detailed and more immediate information. The sales activity could function on its own, but it would be difficult to operate and plan unless the facts of why sales had fallen were known. It was therefore decided that only an active marketing programme, supported by survey research, would provide the direction, guidance and assistance needed to maintain the success of the selling operation. We will see later how this worked out.

## Checklist of key questions for market analysis

*The size of the market*

- What is the size of the total market?
- What is the total value and volume of unit sales?
- What is the value and volume of domestic sales?
- What is the value and volume of export sales?
- What are the sizes of the market segments:
  - by geographical area?
  - by types, quality, version and price of product?
  - by type of distributor and marketing methods?
  - by type of customer in terms of profile and usage?

- What are the substitute product opportunities?
- What are the alternative market opportunities?

*The shape of the market*

- Who are the main manufacturers and suppliers to the market?
- Which are their main markets?
- What are the cyclical variations in these markets?
- What factors will influence competition in the future?
- Who are the main customers and what are their requirements?
- What additional customers could we sell to or service?

*The nature of the market*

- How does this market size compare with 10 years ago, 5 years ago, last year?
- What was the product demand 10 years ago, 5 years ago, last year?
- What trends have emerged from the product demand?
- What changes will influence the market now?
- What customer demands will influence these changes?
- What changes can be achieved by improving our products?
- Which of the trends are likely to change the nature of competition?
- What modern technology can change the nature of the market, the product and manufacturing methods?

*The company share of the market*

- What share of this market do we have?
- What are our competitors' shares?
- What is the company's share of the market segments?
- What are the competitors' shares of these market segments?
- What is the company's share of the various product fields?
- What are the competitors' shares of these product fields?

*The company position in the market*

- What is the company's image amongst the customers?
- What marketing methods are used compared with its competitors?
- How acceptable are these methods to distributors and customers?

## The Effective Use of Market Research

- What new services are required?
- What changes in the company's activity would alter market shape and market share?

# 4

# Researching and Developing New Products

Some managers today view marketing as an essential business tool for the management of change. Whether this change is in the attitudes of consumers or in their purchasing habits, it is important to ensure that products and services being provided meet the needs of those buying them. One of the most effective ways of ensuring that the new situations occurring in the market are being accepted by a company is to pursue an active new product development programme. This type of programme is beneficial if a company finds itself in any of the following situations:

- sales of the current range of products have been declining over a specified period of time.
- information and general feedback from the salesforce about the opinions of distributors, retailers or customers indicate a negative attitude to the current range of products.
- there are complaints from the customers about the products themselves and the internal quality control shows a decline in the standard of the product.
- it is clear that the sale of existing products depends on a higher degree of marketing support than has been provided in the past. This can range from salesforce time in merchandizing products with the distributors, to introducing a new advertising campaign or needing special product promotions to increase consumer awareness.

- major competitors have been successfully modifying their products.

## New product development

The need for a company to research and develop new products naturally results from its desire to increase sales. In practice, new product development is essentially carried out in one of three ways:

1. A company can develop new product features by adapting, modifying, magnifying, minimizing, substituting, rearranging or combining the existing features of a product.
2. A company can create different quality versions of the product. In this way production of the basic product can continue but with variations created to meet the needs of different markets. Leading car manufacturers conduct their marketing in this way.
3. A company can develop and manufacture additional models and sizes.

The checklist on p 58 lists the questions that have to be answered when a company is deciding to carry out new product development.

There are numerous examples of companies who have achieved successful product development activities for products that we buy today, some of which have been researched very carefully in the marketplace, such as the Ford Escort car and Cadbury's *Wispa* chocolate bar.

## Product development and market research

Nevertheless, product development through market research is not as straightforward as it seems. Situations can arise which cause problems and can detract from successful conclusions of some projects. It is important, therefore, to select criteria carefully for the development of market and product opportunities to ensure they cover all aspects of the business. The criteria should be sufficiently detailed to assess:

- Company and business policy.
- The market: in terms of its size, market growth prospects, effects of economic activity.

- The product: in terms of customer distinction, consumer appeal, number of potential customers.
- The competition: in terms of the actual competitors, the degree of opportunity for price flexibility.
- The company itself: in terms of product compatibility, company strengths, research and development requirements, production, distribution, salesforce motivation.
- Overall financial return: in terms of estimated sales in one to five years, estimated gross profit, marketing investment, capital investment.

Take the example of a supplier of a meat product component. Prior to a very detailed and sophisticated new product development programme the company put together some criteria for assessing the most practical alternatives for allowing the company to diversify in the long term. The alternatives were therefore aimed at:

- securing the existing business base.
- funding the activity within the resources available.
- building on the existing corporate strength.
- providing the required levels of margin and return on captial employed.

The benefit of developing such guidelines is to be able to create possible strategic alternatives into which the results of the new product development research could be fed. Such alternatives may include opportunities based on:

- existing corporate resources
- technical expertise
- synergy with the existing business.

One problem that can occur is in the degree of commitment to the product development activity. The development of new product prototypes in some sectors, such as the food and automotive industries, is an expensive and time-consuming activity. Indeed, some companies try to develop them cheaply and quickly and in doing so fail to achieve a standard that is worth developing any further. This may also occur because the new products being developed have to be manufactured according to safety standards; production incorporating these safety features still needs to be cost effective.

Many new product ideas and opportunities are lost or missed because marketing management fails to think ahead as to how the product will be presented to the market or the potential customers. The development of branding and product packaging must be done well in advance, as there is a danger that left too late it will not be in synergy with the product's image and its benefits as perceived by the customers.

It is also important to consider the position of the product in the market when planning the research for the development programme. The key question to answer in this situation is what the product has to equal or surpass in functional terms. This depends on the type of product and the type of brand. The various types are as follows:

- *If the product is a leading brand*
  The product probably needs to achieve parity with its established competition on the market.
- *If the product is a secondary or new brand*
  The product should aim to achieve parity with the brand leader.
- *If the product is a reformulated or redesigned version of an existing brand*
  The product should aim to be at least as acceptable as its current version.
- *If it is a new product*
  The market research undertaken to assess customer needs, and the subsequent launch in the marketplace, should show no evidence of a new product failing to satisfy.

## New product development research procedures

The usual sequence of activities for new product development research is as follows:

1. Initially, ideas for new products are developed through a 'brain-storming session' in which all levels of management think about the type of products the company is capable of producing. Ideas can also be generated through qualitative market research by testing out some of them with the target market. In this way it is possible for the market to set the priorities for the development of the new products. Such priorities take into account those products which are most appealing in the short term and those which have more opportunity

in the longer term.

2.  Once the product concepts have been generated it is then important to set up a full analysis of the business opportunities as well as to develop criteria for new products. On completion of the concept evaluation and the scoring of the products against the set criteria, the highest scoring successful products can be handed to the research and development department to be finalized for manufacture.

3.  The research and development department will then produce prototypes of the final product including the key attributes established through the acceptance of the product concept. These prototypes should be as representative of the final product as possible to ensure that they can be researched and tested under normal conditions.

4.  A full consumer test can then be carried out with a representative sample of the target market for the product. This can be done in one of two ways:

    ●  either through a consumer evaluation in a hall test – a test set up in a public hall or hotel, or pub room, where passers-by are asked to review the product under test conditions; or

    ●  through 'in-home placement' – a product test conducted in participants' homes rather than a central location. In this test the target consumer is invited to try the product as he would use it in an everyday situation.

5.  The names of the product, which would have been discussed at the concept stage, would then need to be tested in the market and matched with the other data on the consumers' acceptance and preferences. These tests could be completed through word association tests, learning tests and name preference tests, all of which can be used to develop a brand name.

6.  Packaging designers can then be commissioned to produce packaging concepts. These would be evaluated either through qualitative group discussions or quantitative hall tests to identify which type of packaging is most acceptable to the potential consumers.

7.  The product is then ready to be marketed.

## Market testing

It is at this stage that one of the most important phases of a market research project should be carried out: market testing, the launch of a new product or service in a limited area, enacting on a small scale a planned introductory programme. Market testing, if properly planned, should provide the means of ensuring a successful launch in the marketplace.

The key action points to remember when setting up a test market are:

- How big should the test market be?
- How many products should be tested at any one time?
- What should the duration of the test market be?

Market testing tends to be more suited to the consumer goods sectors. However, the main reason why this technique has been less successful in industrial markets is that it is more difficult to organize, mainly due to the high costs of production, the higher unit value of an industrial product, the spread of the market and the difficulty in persuading customers to test the product.

Part of the market testing exercise will be to complete a careful analysis of the sales of the product. This would include:

- Selecting a panel of outlets and monitoring the sales through these stores. The sales analysis would have to take account of the sales of the new product compared with the sales of the existing products on the market analysed over a significant period of time.
- Interviewing the purchasers of these products to ascertain why they have bought the product, why they have bought it for a second time and, indeed, why they will or will not buy it again.

**Two cases studies**

The example of Devro Ltd provides an interesting case. The company's activities had concentrated on providing information for its existing markets and how it could get closer to these markets by understanding their attitudes, needs and preferences more clearly.

While other new collagen product opportunities were under examination, the sausage market gave the company a further expansion of its business. Through the research completed in 'sausage user and attitude studies', it had been established that sausages were eaten regularly by most families and that ways of expanding the market would prove difficult. Such a problem posed the following questions:

- How could the number of families eating sausages be increased when 67 per cent of homes already ate them at least once a month and 85 per cent of homes ate them every three months?
- How could the number of occasions when sausages were eaten be increased when they were already a regular meal?
- How could the quantity eaten be increased when the average consumption was already high?

Clearly the analyses of consumption against economic trends and the picture gained from the user and attitude studies showed that sausage was a staple food and to increase the market size would be difficult. There was, however, a clear indication that sausages had become a dinner/tea food and that breakfast use had declined. Further research into this trend identified that cooked breakfasts were only consumed when people had the time available to prepare and eat them. Clearly, in today's high speed society people spend less time preparing for work in the early morning and tend to skip breakfast.

In parallel with these research studies, the company's research and development staff had been investigating methods of preparing sausage. One particular concept was linked directly with the research findings – a pre-cooked, ready-to-reheat sausage which, when combined with bacon, provides a ready-to-eat breakfast.

Extensive research using group discussions, hall tests, and home placements had proved that this concept was not only an acceptable method of preparing breakfast but, if available, would encourage those who have given up the breakfast habit to return to eating a cooked breakfast.

The overall result of this research will be a stimulation of the market by 8 per cent per annum, since the recreation of the breakfast habit would not impinge on the use of sausage at other meal occasions, as the research showed these uses to be discrete eating occasions using a basic staple food.

Another example is the launch of a new range of savoury snacks. The introduction of the *Preludes* range of savoury snacks by Golden Wonder, in the autumn of 1985, represented an important diversification for the company. It was their first attempt to market a range of products aimed specifically at in-home entertaining.

The combined crisp and savoury snack market in the UK was then worth around £800 million. Golden Wonder felt that a market of this size should be capable of sustaining a range of 'premium-priced' products designed for family entertaining occasions. The product enjoyed a successful reception from both trade and consumers.

The company had identified that the market for snacks suitable for home entertaining was very diffuse. Brands such as Phileas Fogg, and European brands such as Bahlsen and Belin, were in limited distribution and in fact the main competitor appeared to be Marks & Spencer.

Market research was identified as necessary to test out the following hypotheses:

- consumers feel that currently there is an insufficient choice of adult savoury snacks
- people are more selective when buying snacks for entertaining
- there is a latent demand for more imaginative savoury snacks for serving to adults
- the market for adult snacks is not particularly price sensitive
- adult snack usage occasions occur with sufficient frequency to justify launching a brand specifically for this sector.
- the Golden Wonder name has sufficient status to carry a range of premium-priced savoury snacks.

Extensive use was made of qualitative research through group discussions during the research. In fact, a total of eight research programmes was completed by Golden Wonder prior to the launch of *Preludes*. Only two of these projects were then quantified, a product test and a price modelling study, designed to test how the demand for the product would vary with a change in price. The company had used the qualitative research for its flexibility, its diagnostic value, its sensitivity and its creativeness.

The initial research results were very encouraging as the various hypotheses were all favourably substantiated.

What happened next had a significant bearing on the successful launch of the *Preludes* range. Golden Wonder formed a project team whose sole objective was to bring this new brand to fruition. This team was led by a senior company manager and the new product development manager. The disciplines included in the team were advertising, production, research and pack design. So, there was a group of committed people who had been set a singular objective of getting the brand to the marketplace, following the encouraging initial qualitative research results.

An important issue in the early stages was to develop a pack design which would reflect the desired positioning, eg:

> 'At last you can give your guests something to nibble with their drinks.'
> 'Golden Wonder now introduce an exciting new range of savoury snacks; each variety is packaged in its own special box to guarantee freshness.'
> 'They are a real treat for home entertaining or even more informal occasions with the family.'

By using a boxed presentation for the new product it was perceived by consumers as being more 'up-market'; the problem was how to avoid going too 'up-market'. The company was also interested in developing a year-round business as opposed to holidays and special occasions, to achieve the optimum sales volumes.

During the course of the research programme, all the key hypotheses were confirmed as the project gained momentum. There were indeed not enough adult snacks around when it came to in-home entertaining. The market did appear to be relatively price insensitive. The products themselves sampled well and the price modelling research provided clear guidelines on just how far it would be possible to go on this particular variable.

Throughout most of the research programme, the brand name *Starters* was felt to be the most suitable option. It was described as 'classy without being pretentious' and 'decidedly adult'. There was just some disquiet from AB consumers in the South East who felt it was a 'bit ordinary'. As a result, other brand name candidates were brought forward, such as *Siennas*, *Folios*, and *Preludes*. Further research was conducted on pack graphics and brand name alternatives. Both *Starters* and *Preludes* fitted the desired positioning but on balance *Preludes* seemed to have an added value edge over *Starters*. One particular comment rather clinched it for *Preludes*:

> 'It reminds me in a way of *After Eight* mints – *Preludes* will stick in my mind.'

This shows how research, through a systematic product development programme, can help to measure the extent to which a company's product or range of products meets the standards of consumer acceptance set for it. These standards must be established by marketing and research management developing new products by determining how the new product relates to existing products on the market, competition, product development and the perceived needs of the potential customers.

### Checklist of questions on researching and developing new products

The key questions that have to be answered when a company is deciding to carry out product development are:

- How well are our products doing?
- Do we need to modify our products?
- Do we need additional products in the product range?
- What products do our customers need?
- What product modifications are feasible in our production capabilities and within our financial resources?
- What product opportunities are feasible in our production capabilities and within our financial resources?
- How many models can we have in our range?
- How many sizes can we have in our range?
- How does the consumer/buyer react to the proposed changes in our products, or towards the new product?
- What other modifications/new features are acceptable to our customers or potential customers depending on the resources available?

# 5

# Monitoring the Success of a Product

Once a product has been launched in the marketplace, its success as judged by sales achieved can be monitored, but its ultimate success depends on building up a realistic and acceptable image, which takes time. Enhancing the product's image can be achieved by giving the product a brand identity, by ensuring that all aspects of communications about the product to customers create, stimulate and maintain the demand for the product. This brand identity could be extended through the name of the product, the colour and design of the product's packaging, the communications and promotional messages used in advertising and sales promotion. It is important to evaluate how well a brand's image is perceived by consumers by monitoring the success of a product in the marketplace through market research.

The monitoring process is based on the following questions:

- What is the image of the product?
- How well has our product been selling in the last six months, or in the last year?
- What is our brand share?
- What is our market penetration?
- Are our marketing activities sufficient to hold our brand shares?

(A full checklist to assist in monitoring the success of a product is given on p 64.)

It is realistic to point out that a number of companies believe that the initial development of a brand's image is sufficient and that no further additional research is required to find out how to maintain the brand's market share. However, it must be realized that it is often the customers' evaluation of the brand which helps a company decide what marketing activities are required in the future. Stimulation of product sales may only be achieved by new selling and merchandizing activities. Equally, distributors may become more attracted to competitive brands, so trade incentives may be required.

Typical situations which indicate that product or service monitoring is required are:

- When a company has identified through its sales figures that its brand share is falling and indeed its products have a poor or diminishing penetration of the market. This may be of great concern, particularly if the brand share is falling at a time when the total marketing activity is being maintained at a constant level.
- Where a company is finding it difficult to get the distribution it requires for its products, because other brands or competitive brands are achieving a better share and a better distribution.
- Where competition is investing heavily in 'above the line activity' to support or stimulate the sales of other brands.
- Where current marketing activity, particularly advertising, is achieving little or no response in terms of increased sales.
- Where feedback from both distribution in the trade and consumers purchasing the brand is poor in relation to the acceptance of the product and the communication methods used to create product awareness.

Continuous monitoring should alert management at an early stage to problems such as these, so that remedial action based on the research can be taken.

However, those companies that have evaluated their product's image further have experienced a number of problems which the marketing or research manager wanting to complete a brand evaluation needs to be aware of. These include:

- failing to ensure that the research on the product is completed to a specification to which all those involved in the sales and promotion of the product can adhere.
- some companies have experienced problems due to factors beyond

their own and their research house's control. For example, the point-of-sale positioning of the brand chosen by the retailer or wholesaler during the period of the research may not be ideal for maximum exposure to the customer.

- failing to look at all the marketing activities being carried out at the time of the research and take into account the effects that the activities have on the results of the research. For example, it is easy to overlook what advertising and sales activities are being used and what stage they are at in their implementation. An increase in sales from the success of the advertising and merchandising campaigns supported with a specific sales effort by the sales representatives, could cause the research results to be very misleading.
- failing to assess carefully other influences that could affect the evaluation and analysis of the research. These are mainly concerned with the marketing and sales activities of the company's competitors, which may not be representative of the usual activities in the market.

## The monitoring sequence

The usual sequence of activities for carrying out research on brand standing is as follows:

1. Setting up all the requirements of the research by:
   - deciding on the objectives of the research
   - setting the criteria against which the product evaluation should take place and on what scale and for how long
   - organizing a full research programme designed to monitor movements in the market.
2. Selecting test locations for the products. This would require searching for the data on the most appropriate sales areas, test towns, supermarket or other outlets and ITV or independent local radio areas.
3. Finding out, assessing and evaluating what other marketing activities the company and its competitors are currently carrying out.
4. Organizing a research programme which can provide a measurement of sales in the market, thus providing the estimate for brand standing. This would require collecting data on the sale of brands in the market and comparing sales figures.

**61**

5. Setting up or buying into either a retail audit – a method of obtaining information about the movement of products into and out of retail outlets – or a consumer panel – a sample of individuals whose purchases and product usage are recorded over a period – to monitor consumer reactions to the product. The retail audit will provide information on consumer sales and brand shares in terms of units sold, sterling value, average per shop handling, retailer purchases, source of delivery, retailer stocks, stock cover, prices and promotion. A consumer panel, however, will provide information on consumer purchases and brand share in terms of units sold, sterling value, brand penetration, consumer demographics, consumer psychographic characteristics, buying behaviour such as where purchases are made, the prices, and promotion and advertising.

## Case study – the sausage market again

Returning again to Devro Ltd – the earlier chapters told of the company's interest in establishing why sales had dropped. Although the company had defined the size, shape and nature of the sausage and sausage casing markets, it still needed research which would provide the direction, guidance and assistance needed to maintain the success of the selling operation.

The next phase of its research aimed to obtain basic information on the characteristics of the sausage market and subsequently answer the following questions:

- Who are sausage buyers?
- Where are sausage buyers?
- How often do they buy sausages?
- Why do they buy sausages?
- When do they eat sausages?
- Who in the family eats sausages?

In this way, the characteristics of the sausage market could be appreciated and considered along with the changing patterns of the market.

The only information the company had access to regarding customers' attitudes to its casings and how they compared with competitors, was that supplied to the marketing department from the salesmen. This information was mainly based on reports on what the manufacturers were saying about the sales of specific types of sausages. It was therefore essential to complement the existing research of some years before by designing market research to evaluate consumers' attitudes not only towards the sausages and their casings but to the casings themselves.

Initially, the research seemed complex as the problem lay in ensuring that the company did not compare sausages and identify the preferences towards them. However, research techniques, such as product testing in halls, together with paired-comparison techniques (a product test in which people are asked to compare two products), were to prove successful using a specifically designed and structured questionnaire to incorporate the key characteristics of both sausages and casings, explored initially through group discussions.

The sausage encased in various types of casing takes on different shapes, textures and colours, although the consistency of the sausage may be the same in terms of its ingredients, recipe, manufacture and texture. By putting together attribute statements about the sausage and its casing, the research company were able to compare and identify preferences for sausages and their casings.

The attribute statements listed on the questionnaires included:

- attractive shape
- pleasant colour
- uniform size
- pleasing taste
- meaty appearance
- nice texture
- easy to bite
- easy to chew

and the statements were rated by using a five point scale, from 'agree strongly' to 'disagree strongly'.

The product tests that were carried out in this phase were:

- a comparison of casings made for sausage manufacturers for use on their high-speed linking sausage filling machines
- a comparison of casings made for butchers for use on their hand linking sausage filling machines
- a comparison of coarse and fine mixtures and their effect on casing qualities.

**63**

The result of this initial research phase was that Devro Ltd were able to compare preferences for sausages in different casings and identify these preferences in terms of shape, appearance, and edibility.

More importantly, the results created two key opportunities:

1. salesmen could provide customers with factual information on consumer preferences for collagen casing
2. potential customers could be assured that the traditional use of animal gut for the manufacture of sausage casings was not a consumer preference, giving them the opportunity of productivity gains and enhanced sausage product characteristics.

This research therefore became the basis for monitoring the market. It was also realized that although the company had data on the consumers' preferences for its casing on the sausage product, it needed to monitor regularly the movements in the market. Using the attitudes statements and the basic questions shown earlier in the chapter as a model, an annual 'user and attitude' survey was set up to assess the trends in the sausage market. This annual survey then became the means of monitoring the success of the market and the company's products in the market.

**Checklist of questions for monitoring the success of a product**

- What is our share of the market?
- What is our market penetration?
- Which distribution channel should we concentrate on?
- How well has the product been selling?
- What marketing support is there in the market?
- What is the image of the product?
- Who are our product's buyers?
- Where are our product's buyers?
- How often do they buy the product?
- Why do they buy the product?

# 6

# Developing Marketing Communications

One of the most interesting aspects of marketing is the communications process and how it is used to make potential buyers more interested in and more prepared to buy a product. Many companies try to justify the investment in communications by identifying an immediate increase in sales, market share or international competitiveness. This investment can only be worthwhile if all elements of the marketing mix are working in synergy. Thus, communications have to be carefully planned and monitored and the development needs to be staged in a similar way to the internal preparation described in previous chapters.

The objectives of a communications campaign are as follows:

- To make potential customers aware of a new product or service.
- To indicate new uses of a product or service already on the market.
- To remind existing customers of a product to help to maintain their loyalty to it.
- To provide details on product attributes.
- To initiate sales by generating enquiries.
- To increase awareness amongst wholesalers, retailers and other distributors.
- To develop a corporate image for the company.
- To inform customers and distributors of price changes, special offers and other important marketing information.

The methods of marketing communications encompass:

- Advertising: TV, radio, in national newspapers, local newspapers, consumer magazines, trade magazines, free newsheets, posters, stations, airports, trains, taxis, etc.
- Sales promotion: competitions, vouchers, in-store demonstrations, displays, trade shows, industry exhibitions, etc.
- Public relations: articles, editorials, presentations, information sheets, brochures and any material which provides information on the product or service to customers, potential customers, influencers and even, in some interesting situations, competitors.
- Personal selling: the defined and planned approach used by the salesforce to communicate the benefits of the products to potential buyers, to persuade them to buy the product rather than competitors' products.

The emphasis or 'slant' of communications changes according to the various stages of the product life cycle as follows:

- *'awareness and knowledge'* for the introduction of a product: the types of communications used for this will include announcements, descriptive copy, classified advertisements, slogans, jingles and any other forms of 'teasers'.
- *'liking and preference'* for the growth and maturity of a product: the types of communications used for these include competitive advertising and 'image' advertisements.
- *'conviction and purchase'* for the saturation and declining stage of a product: the types of communications used for these include point-of-sale displays, in-store advertising, special offers, etc.

There are many other books which describe the techniques of communications and how they are developed by companies. In this chapter we will only examine how research can ensure that the advertising being developed has the required 'synergy' to be an effective component of the marketing mix.

The basic role of any type of communications is to reach a 'target audience' with the defined messages to change or reinforce their attitudes and also to influence their behaviour. Communications therefore need to be planned effectively. (A checklist of questions for communications planning is given on p 70.)

Market research has an important part to play in the development and monitoring of communications. As indicated earlier, it is very difficult for management to evaluate through research the complete contribution of advertising and other communications, as they are all part of the marketing mix. Research can, however, make a positive contribution to the development of advertising. The typical sequence for the use of research would be to:

- Identify the most profitable market for the product or service. The potential for the product must be evaluated and then quantified so that there is clear data on the consumers' buying decisions, the manufacturing technical requirements for the product, social and economic characteristics, and other psychological, personal, and environmental issues that are involved.
- Determine the product's basic characteristics. A technique such as motivation research – discovering reasons for people's behaviour – will identify what the potential customer's existing attitudes to products in the market are. It is also useful for assessing consumers' reasons for holding these attitudes. This will help to identify which of the product's characteristics match the consumers' needs and pre-conceived attitudes to the products.
- Test out the appropriate marketing strategy.
- Test out what should be included in the advertising and how it should be communicated.
- Monitor the results of both the advertising and the marketing.

## Case study

Take for example the development of the advertising campaign for John Smith's bitter in Yorkshire. Research enabled the company to identify the nature of the brand's problems and the reasons behind them. In addition, it helped to define the role of advertising and provide guidance for the creation of a specific campaign solution and then monitor its effects. In this situation John Smith's decisions were constantly made with reference to the needs of the consumers, their attitudes and their reactions to the product. Consequently, an advertising campaign was developed that also made a contribution to the company's profits.

The beer market is a very large and competitive market and was in decline at the time of this campaign. In the fight for brand share the UK brewers spent heavily on advertising, with over £40 million being spent on TV alone in 1981, the year the John Smith campaign began. Company sales and market audit data showed that the brand had been losing volume for a year or more, particularly in tied pubs in Yorkshire. The market share lost by the company was estimated to be worth £2 million, together with the related retailing profit on the pubs' non-beer sales and general custom.

Diagnosis of John Smith's falling sales indicated a consumer problem with the brand. Other potential causes of the problem were eliminated, as the product had not been changed in any way; its price was in line with competing products; its distribution had not declined; there was no evidence of the falling standards of the pubs; there was no problem with the staff; and no other product had been promoted at the expense of the 'bitter' product. It was only its presentation that had been slightly modified a few years earlier, but up until then there had been no indication that this could have been the cause of the problem.

Analysis of existing survey data revealed the symptoms of John Smith's decline. The brand had been losing loyal drinkers, particularly the younger drinkers. The data showed that competition was gaining these drinkers.

Qualitative research was commissioned with John Smith's drinkers and competitive product drinkers. The results of this research suggested that the John Smith's brand lacked 'character'. It failed to arouse enthusiasm amongst its drinkers and was thought of merely as 'one of Yorkshire's bitters'. In fact the young drinker thought of it as 'an old boy's pint' and compared it unfavourably with competing brands. This contrast in attitude to the two brands was in turn confirmed by a quantitative survey.

Further research also identified:

- There had been a change in the market, as drinkers were now being offered hand-pumped, cask-conditioned ales. The younger drinkers were particularly interested in these.
- John Smith, in the past, had been stressing the brand's Yorkshire heritage, and more recently other bitters had also made similar claims. The group discussions had shown that the drinkers had become confused as to which brand was responsible for which advertising. In addition, young drinkers were looking to lager

advertising for originality, fun and youthfulness, as they found the bitter advertising to be dull and old-fashioned.

The qualitative research also identified a connection between advertising and brand choice due to the importance of the 'imagery' of beers, particularly amongst young drinkers. Drinking is a social activity, and group pressures can be strong. The public selection of a brand of beer reflects the buyer's self-image in the same way as his choice of clothes. The under 30s tend not to be beer experts, but do seek a brand that reflects them as knowledgeable drinkers. They are influenced by what is popular and fashionable with their 'peer' group. The younger drinkers also provide a target group as they drink more than older men and they use a wider repertoire of pubs and consume a greater range of drinks. The tastes they develop at an early stage will be retained and will determine the future make-up of the market. The most volatile group in terms of brand imagery and choice, the 18–24 age group, are also the most susceptible to fashion and the most interested in and responsive to advertising. They therefore became the primary target for the company.

In this instance, it was realized that restoring drinkers' commitment to John Smith's bitter would be a swift and inexpensive way of achieving increased sales, in comparison to the alternatives of installing new brewing and bar dispensing facilities for hand-pumped cask bitter, or even increasing the investment in John Smith's pubs. What was needed, at a time when lager advertising was the most empathetic to young drinkers, and hand pumps were becoming the symbols of good bitter, was an advertising campaign which expressed John Smith's personality that would revive confidence in the brand.

In order to develop the advertising group discussions were carried out. Forty groups were completed over two years in different towns in Yorkshire. They were divided into:

- initial exploratory work
- evaluation of competitive campaigns
- strategic concept testing
- exposure of creative ideas
- post-testing of finished commercials.

The creative solution was the 'Big John' idea. 'A pint of John's' is how the brand is often ordered at the bar and to this affectionate nickname was added the image of John Smith's as a 'big' pint – flavourful, strong, popular, successful and as right today as it has ever been.

The launch of the campaign restored the bitter's share of advertising awareness in the county. Qualitative research in 1981 organized to post-test the first advertising suggested that the desired communication was being achieved. Drinkers vastly enjoyed the advertising and seemed to derive meaning from it. The brand's status was higher and the drinkers seemed to be more committed to it. Thus the brand's sales turn-around was accompanied by improvements in the measures which had led the company to identify John Smith's problem as a consumer problem. By conducting accurate qualitative research the advertising could be connected with behaviour and thus determined the role and nature of the advertising. Advertising proved a profitable investment in this case, as it was guided by usable market and advertising research.

## Checklist of questions for communications planning

- Which target audience do we want to communicate with?
- What communication are we going to use?
- Which media is the most cost effective way of communicating with this audience?
- When is the most beneficial time to communicate with this audience?
- How much will it cost us to communicate in this way?
- How will we measure the results of the advertising?

# 7

# Monitoring the Success of an Advertising Campaign

We have seen in the previous chapter how advertising is clearly linked with all marketing issues and very much part of the 'marketing mix'. Advertising is only one part of the marketing mix that leads to a sale, with product characteristics, availability, price, packaging, sales promotion, merchandising and point-of-purchase displays all making an important contribution. Quite often the contribution of advertising to the success of a company's marketing is wrongly assessed: the fundamental workings of the marketing mix achieve the success a company wants in its sales, but it is the impact of an advertising campaign that takes the credit for this success. It is important, therefore, to qualify the use of advertising in the marketing mix.

Marketing management is concerned with using advertising to reach a target audience, whether consumers, the trade, specifiers, purchasers or others, with messages aimed at changing or reinforcing their attitudes as well as influencing their behaviour. Market research has an important part to play in:

- identifying the market for the product or service.
- assessing which of the product or service characteristics are most appealing to the market.
- developing the appropriate marketing strategy to launch the product or service.
- determining what should be communicated in the advertising, as seen in the previous chapter.

- assessing the results of selected marketing and advertising strategies over a period of time.

There are a number of techniques available for researching advertising. Media, reader, TV, and radio audience research and research into the communication of the advertising's words and copy are all important diagnostic tools. They do not, however, measure the effectiveness of the advertising in terms of the degree to which people's knowledge and attitudes may have been changed, improved or even confused by the advertising.

A checklist for monitoring the success of an advertising campaign is given on p. 77.

## Case study

Take as an example the cigarette market. In the late 1970s the market underwent an important change in that the UK tobacco tax structure was harmonized with that of the rest of the EEC. The effect of this change was the elimination of the difference in price between cigarettes of different sizes, and the scene was set for growth of the King Size sector, which then quickly dominated the market.

The change in the 'market shape' presented problems for Imperial Tobacco, which had dominated the medium and small sized cigarette markets, but was under-represented in the King Size sector. The company's first priority was to establish King Size versions of their medium and small size brand leaders. Thus Embassy No 1, Regal King Size and No 6 King Size were launched with the strategic aim of creating a natural haven for smokers of these brands at King Size.

By 1979 these King Size line extensions were well established and the company was looking for a new brand that would compete more directly against competitive brands such as Benson & Hedges and Rothmans which had the advantage of purely King Size heritage.

New brand concepts were then researched and the most popular one to emerge was the King Size version of John Player Special International. The original brand had been launched in 1972 as something slightly beyond the mainstream of King Size brands. The brand had the flat two-row pack, offered a slightly longer than King Size product and was charged at a premium price. This formula had been successful, but it also proved to be a source of weakness in the long run, as the brand had become classified by consumers as a 'special occasions only' product, with a limited sales volume potential.

Imperial Tobacco's research showed a high awareness of the brand and admiration for the black and gold pack. The concept tests showed a very high level of consumer interest in a conventional King Size version of John Player Special – with the normal three-row box, standard King Size dimensions and a price that was competitive with regular King Size brands.

Given that these basic elements in the brand's make-up were going to be changed, an important decision had to be taken about how to treat the other major elements in the brand presentation, ie the surface design of the pack and the advertising. Should they be modified to reflect the new positioning or should they be kept consistent with the parent brand presentation to carry over the quality and luxury associations of the original John Player Special?

The company's advertising agency began a review of all the available consumer research about the original John Player Special brand. The original JPS advertising had been deliberately up-market, using expensive status symbols to reinforce the brand's quality and luxury associations. The review suggested that the advertising stance might have exacerbated the inherent problems of the unconventional pack versus size versus price format – taking the exclusivity to the point where the brand seemed totally out of reach to most smokers. The research also showed that the original advertising was seen as 'taking itself too seriously' and so it was decided to introduce a more human touch through the use of humour. In this case a series of advertisements were developed based on the word 'black'. The idea was researched, and it was shown that the advertising, which reflected the original John Player Special style, still projected a brand that was exclusive, and for special occasions only.

The more relaxed approach of the 'puns' campaign suggested a brand with which a broad cross-section of the market could identify. It was clear that it was unnecessary to add expensive props to a pack that already looks as expensive as John Player Special.

A further problem was that advertising reminiscent of the original John Player Special brand's style failed to make it clear that this was a new brand launch. The 'puns' campaign carried much less risk of people missing the new brand point, as it proved to be a clear break with the past. It was decided to adopt the 'puns' approach as the campaign theme for the new brand.

The original launch advertising consisted of a three-stage approach:

- A simple announcement advertisement, showing little more than the pack on a white background, so as to concentrate emphasis on the copy points of 'new' King Size and price.
- A mono campaign with the same simple pack visual, using black 'pun' headlines such as 'put 60p on the black', 'hardly blackmail' to stress the introductory price/value message, but in a witty manner relating to the main media theme.
- The main theme campaign, which ran in colour and showed the pack photographed in a real-life situation with black 'pun' headlines, such as 'pocket the black' on a snooker table, and 'blackgammon' with a backgammon board.

The post-launch monitoring research showed very satisfactory levels of brand recall and advertising recall. Nevertheless, the company had seen other new launches achieve good recall, only to lose their impact soon afterwards. Therefore further exploratory research was commissioned to assess consumers' response in depth and to examine the directions which future advertising might take.

This research raised some questions on the type of decisions that could be taken. There appeared to be two potential disadvantages with these 'pack in real life' visuals:

- The nature of the scene shown tended to position the brand towards one social class or another, for example, up-market with backgammon, down-market with snooker. Neither implication was appropriate in a market which was rapidly becoming one size, one price, nor for a brand which was capable of usage among a very broad cross-section of smokers.
- While the black pack and the black pun headlines were distinctive, the 'pack in situ' visual was closer to the stock-in-trade of cigarette advertising. In effect, it failed to provide a unique look for the advertising which the company and the consumers themselves felt would be right for such a unique brand.

The key to the direction for John Player Special's advertising development was provided by the pre-test results for some subjects that were originally conceived simply as posters. In these advertisements, the original advertising idea was stripped down to the bare essentials of the black pun and the black pack, using an abstract style of visual with a pack or packs arranged geometrically on a white background and a single, very simple line. These advertisements consisted of subjects like 'black and front' with the pack shot from back and front, and 'short black and sides', with similarly appropriate shots of the pack.

From the earliest exposure in qualitative research with group discussions, these advertisements achieved a very positive response. The reasons for this were not simply the appreciation of the humour, but also because:

- they were quite unlike any other cigarette advertisements that had been seen before, while still being self-evidently cigarette advertisements with the product itself in the 'starring role and relegated to obscurity.'
- they make the most of the unique black pack which was the essence of John Player Special's appeal. They did so by removing all other pictorial elements from the advertising except the pack, instead of the conventional solution of building a scene around it.
- in the absence of any other indicators, the advertising was totally sexless, classless and timeless. Men were at liberty to see the brand as masculine and women to see it as chic and so forth, according to taste.
- the smoker projected his or her interests on to the brand, using simply the pack as the indicator. The advertising did not seem to be trying to classify the brand or its smokers.

Two lessons were learnt in the months that followed the introductory campaign. Initially consumers were capable of seeing and indeed wished to see a visible and coherent style in the brand's advertising. What consumers primarily remembered John Player advertising for was a certain style that could be described in general terms – plain and simple, black and white, focused on the pack, witty play on words, etc. Thus the campaign had begun to take on a life of its own and indeed smokers began to claim recall of black pun lines which had never appeared.

Consumer research showed that appreciation of John Player Special advertising could be on any one of three different levels for a particular consumer:

- there was the common denominator, those who appreciated clear display of the pack itself and were also oblivious of any greater subtlety in the advertisements.
- there were those people who appreciated the puns as easily recognizable from common sayings.
- there were those who were actually personally involved with the advertising who waited to see the new advertising.

It was established that each individual advertisement, simple as it might be, was capable of a far greater degree of exposure than had initially been supposed. This was again apparent in quantitative terms in that the recall of any individual cigarette subjects, even for John Player Special, was low in absolute terms. In addition, responses from the group discussions, which included advertisements like 'short, black and sides', still raised chuckles even towards the end of a long discussion session. So the level of exposure for each subject was adjusted until it appeared that the right balance was being achieved between getting maximum value per idea and preserving variety.

The John Player advertising campaign has thus arisen out of very thorough research into market requirements and advertising requirements of what was intended to be the company's most important initiative in the King Size market. Subsequent advertising development has been equally thorough in its use of consumer research. The results were satisfying:

- in demonstrating that research does not need to be a barrier to creativity – as can be seen from looking at the advertisements themselves.
- in achieving unprecedented levels of advertising recall and response, the John Player advertising became the best remembered of any advertising and the most cost-effective in terms of recall per expenditure.
- in terms of sales results, which saw John Player Special achieve the best performance of any new brand in the cigarette market since 1966.

**Checklist of questions for monitoring the success of an advertising campaign**

- What is the awareness of the product, service or advertising campaign we have invested in?
- What is the customer's knowledge of the product or service in terms of its features or benefits?
- What is the image of the product or service in terms of whether the advertising has strengthened or weakened its image?
- How acceptable is the advertising to the consumer?
- Which aspects of the communications messages persuaded the consumer to buy the product or use the company's service?

# 8

# Identifying and Measuring Consumer Attitudes

## The growing importance of marketing

In recent years, consumers have become more discriminating in their purchasing habits; their needs for different products and different brands are constantly changing. Consequently, it has become necessary for both manufacturers and retailers continuously to analyse the needs of their customers and identify how to improve marketing, products and communications to meet these needs more directly.

The marketing of both goods and services is therefore becoming more complex – and extremely sophisticated. As a result the techniques that companies use for deciding on their sales and marketing are changing. In response to rapidly changing markets, the current trend is for companies to be 'market-driven' rather than 'sales-driven': ie, having analysed the needs of their customers, companies can then set targets which relate to known factors in the marketplace. In this way companies become closer to the market and are more prepared for managing change.

So, with management becoming more oriented towards both their markets and their customers, companies are adopting programmes which are designed to:

- appreciate the nature of consumer behaviour by understanding how such behaviour is affected by social, cultural, psychological and economic factors.
- examine the importance of influencing factors such as groups,

**79**

families, or population changes which may affect consumer behaviour and subsequent buying decisions.

● understand the nature of consumer decision-making processes and how they relate to buying choice.

Management is increasingly using new techniques to understand how consumers react to marketing and other influences on their behaviour. The task for the manager is to interpret these reactions, referred to as 'buyers' responses'. It is, therefore, important for the manager to assess both behaviour patterns and consumer characteristics. Indeed, consumer behaviour is influenced by the buyer's characteristics and by the buyer's decision-making process.

## Assessing consumer buying behaviour

Consumer buying behaviour is influenced by:

● *The culture in which the consumer lives*
Consumers have values, perceptions, preferences and a behaviour pattern which are the result of environmental influences. Leisure habits, health factors and life style have as important an influence on buying behaviour as religion and nationality. Research helps to track cultural shifts that might suggest new ways to market and sell to consumers. Analysis of the different cultural life styles also helps to identify both product and brand preferences.

● *The social classification of the consumer*
Consumer sub-cultures are classified by their patterns of occupation, income, education, wealth and other variables which can be used to distinguish between different types of people. Research helps to develop marketing and sales campaigns that are targeted at the special attitudes, needs and perceptions of the different sub-groups. This kind of classification also proves to be useful in identifying the differences in the buying behaviour between males and females in a family. For example, research shows that husbands tend to be dominant in taking decisions on life insurance, the choice of car and what TV programmes to watch. Wives tend to be dominant in the choice of washing machine, carpeting and kitchenware. Husbands and wives make joint decisions when choosing living room furniture, where to go on holiday and where to live.

- *The personal characteristics of the consumer*
  The consumer's age, life-cycle stage, occupation, economic circumstances and personality influence the way in which he or she takes buying decisions. Research assists in identifying consumer lifestyles and provides management with the key to satisfying their needs. The VALS (values and lifestyles) classification, developed in the US, is an example of how people can be categorized through research, according to their life styles and personal characteristics:

  *'survivors'* – people who find little satisfaction in life and just live from day to day

  *'sustainers'* – people striving for a better life and hoping for a better status

  *'belongers'* – people who accept their life styles and tend to follow the example of others, rather than provide a lead

  *'emulators'* – people who are striving to progress and emulate those who have more money and more success than they do

  *'achievers'* – hard working, successful people who exude self-confidence and communicate satisfaction in achieving their goals

  *'I am me'* – people who are in a transition, looking for new interests and new goals in their lives

  *'experientials'* – more intense people who appreciate nature and look for the spiritual meaning in their existence and daily lives

  *'socially conscious'* – people concerned about social issues like pollution, and who are sophisticated and political

  *'integrateds'* – people who lead and set an example to others.

- *The psychological influences on the consumer*
  It is important for management to analyse what motivates consumers by assessing their image and perceptions of a company, identifying how they become aware of products and how their attitudes are changed by advertising and communications.

## Researching behavioural characteristics of the consumer

Getting to know the needs of the consumer almost guarantees success in marketing. Determining how buyers go through the decision-making process provides marketing management with all they need to know

**81**

about selling a product the consumer wants to buy. It can be useful to build a predictive model of the behaviour of an individual. The information required to build and illustrate the model includes:

- the behaviour, beliefs and attitudes of consumers
- the extent to which they are aware of choices
- the importance they attach to different product brand characteristics
- any constraints that might exist on buying behaviour.

In assessing consumer buying behaviour, then, the most important research activities are:

- to collect and analyse data relating to the habits, attitudes and needs of consumers, with a view to sorting consumers into homogeneous groups differentiated by their life styles and buying behaviour.
- to collect and analyse data relating to the products, services or brands that are available in the market. This helps to focus on how these are perceived by consumers, with a view to sorting the brands into groups of those with 'like attributes' as perceived by the consumer.

## Buyers' characteristics and buying decisions

It is important to identify the characteristics of buyers and their buying decision processes in order to target them with the most appropriate marketing methods. Management need to gain an understanding of how their characteristics and decision-making processes relate to the products or services they choose; the brand they select; the outlet at which they buy the product; the time it takes them to decide which products to buy; and the amount purchased.

To assess how buying decisions are made, it is necessary to identify the criteria used for buying products and the level and type of influence on the buyer.

## Buying roles

Several different roles have been defined in the consumer buying process:

**82**

- the 'initiator' – the first person to think of the idea of buying a particular product
- the influencer – the person who influences others in taking the final decision to purchase
- the decider – the person who takes the key decision
- the buyer – the person who makes the actual purchase
- the user – the consumer or the user.

## Buying behaviour

Buying behaviour divides into different types: routine buying, initial problem solving, and extended problem solving. The marketing response will be different in each case.

### Routine buying

The consumer will be purchasing low cost goods frequently and will not be giving much thought to the purchase he will be making. Marketing management will want to ensure continuing customer satisfaction by maintaining the product's quality, service and value. New customers will also be attracted through promotions which emphasize the product's acceptability and point out its specific features and benefits.

### Initial problem solving

The consumer might be interested in another product brand/product class, but does not know too much about it. He will ask specific questions at the point of sale about the product or will look to advertising and promotions to learn more about its specific features and benefits. An advertising campaign will be created aimed at increasing consumers' awareness and developing product familiarity.

### Extended problem solving

The consumer might be interested in buying a specific product in a product line about which he has little or no knowledge. He has to ascertain what criteria to use in solving the problem of which product to buy. Marketing management needs to understand these criteria to ensure that all communications convey the attributes of the products appreciated by the consumers.

## Examining the purchasing process

The purchasing process can be broken down into five different stages – problem recognition, information search, evaluation of alternatives, the purchasing decision, and post-purchase behaviour.

Research should be carried out at each of these stages, to arm the marketing manager with information and guidance on the most appropriate marketing response for each stage.

### Problem recognition

The initial stage is recognition by the consumer of a need to be filled, or problem to be solved, by the purchase of a product.

Research identifies what needs or problems consumers have, what caused them and how they led to the product being chosen. Gathering this data helps the marketing manager to identify what most often motivates interest in the product category. Then he will be able to develop marketing communications which stimulate the interest.

### Information search

A consumer will absorb information on the product he is going to buy well before doing so. Advertisements, mailshots, looking at similar products owned by friends and other members of the family, all help to determine the attributes of the product. The search for information thus divides into:

- personal sources – talking to friends and neighbours
- commercial sources – looking at advertisements, walking around shops and looking at the displays, or seeking advice from sales staff in a shop
- experiential sources – handling and using the product.

It is in this way that the consumer increases his awareness of the product that he wants to buy.

Research is used by companies marketing the products to identify which sources of information are evaluated and how they are rated. Typical research will assess:

- how consumers first heard about the product and the brands of products
- what information they received

- how they decided to rank the importance of the various information sources
- what criteria were ranked
- what their overall reactions were to the information and how it persuaded them to buy the product.

After this assessment, a company can develop the appropriate communications campaign aimed at its potential markets.

*Evaluation of the alternatives*
Consumers will decide between one product and another by comparing the various characteristics and attributes of the different products. Research techniques are used to encourage consumers to assess:

- the product's attributes
- 'importance weightings' for these attributes
- the consumers' beliefs about the product
- the product's utility functions
- the ways in which consumers evaluate the products and their attributes.

Consumers will obviously pay most attention to the attributes that most closely reflect their needs.

Research helps to identify those market segments which are most likely to be attracted to the particular attributes of a product. It is therefore important to research the motivations of buyers to find out how they actually evaluate product and brand alternatives.

Different marketing responses to consumer product evaluation could be:

- to redesign the product to ensure it has all the characteristics the potential buyer expects and, indeed, needs to ensure that he buys the product
- to change the perception of the product or service, by emphasizing some of its features or benefits
- to change the consumer's beliefs about competitors' brands by emphasizing the benefits of one product over another
- to change the importance 'weights' given to the different product attributes, to show that, for example, the size of the product might bring added benefits to a consumer

**85**

- to emphasize attributes which the potential purchasers do not readily identify.

*Purchasing decision*
Management should also be aware of less predictable influences over the purchasing decision, such as:

- the attitude of others towards the product. For example, a spouse might suggest that a cheaper product or a more expensive product, would be better
- the need to economize, or the opportunity to spend a little more.

*Post-purchase behaviour*
After the product has been bought management needs to know about the customers' reactions and whether or not his expectations were met. Market research at this stage will, of course, establish how effective the marketing and sales operation has been.

## Consumer behaviour classifications

Most market and media research studies collect a mass of data about consumers and their characteristics. Typically, this survey data has been analysed on single dimensions such as age, sex, income, and social class. The purpose of recording such information is to be able to evaluate a consumer in terms of his or her type of purchasing behaviour. The UK social grade classifications of A, B, C1, C2, D, E are based on the occupational status of the head of the household. The value of this classification has been eroded by the increasing number of families with two or more income earners and by the redistribution of income and purchasing power across the classes. This limits the definition of target markets and any further detail has to come from cross-tabulation or segmentation computations which adds to the cost of the research.

To circumvent this problem, a new classification, SAGACITY (a special analysis of the national readership survey), has been developed in the UK.

*SAGACITY*
SAGACITY is a new, single-dimension classification readily tabulated

## Income of Head of Household – Chief Wage Earner

Only informants who are head of household, chief wage earner, or wives of head of household/chief wage earner are asked the income question. Where information is refused or not known, an estimate is made in the office. Up to the end of December 1979, a fixed scale of income groups has been used in the NRS. A new scale has been introduced from January, 1980, which will be updated every half year. This scale is exponential, and its points are so set as to allow for the rate of inflation predicted over the intervening six month period. With such a 'constant price' income scale, the real value of the income groups will remain approximately constant over time.

The figures published for 1980 combine the income data from the two scales January–June, and July–December, 1980. The groups used are shown below.

| Income Code | Income Scales | |
| --- | --- | --- |
| | January June 1980 | July December 1980 |
| 0 | £1,120 | £1,210 |
| 1 | £1,400 | £1,520 |
| 2 | £1,750 | £1,820 |
| 3 | £2,190 | £2,370 |
| 4 | £2,730 | £2,960 |
| 5 | £3,420 | £3,700 |
| 6 | £4,270 | £4,630 |
| 7 | £5,340 | £5,880 |
| 8 | £6,680 | £7,230 |
| 9 | £8,350 or more | £9,040 or more |

**Figure 8.1** Chart of the SAGACITY groupings

| Dependent | | Pre-family | | Fam | |
|---|---|---|---|---|---|
| • Age 15-34 but not HoH/CWE or wife of HoH/CWE<br>• or single full-time student aged 15-34 | | Age 15-34 and HoH/CWE or wife of HoH/CWE<br><br>where household type is adults only; informant has no children 16-20, and is not a full-time student | | Age 15-64 and HoH/C<br><br>where household typ<br>informant has children 16<br>full-t | |
| | | | | **Better Off**<br><br>**ABC1 male**<br>Income codes 8 or 9; and if HoH/CWE and married a⚫ wife is working f/t or p/t 8-2 hrs/w, code 7; and if HoH/CWE and married ar wife is working f/t, code 6.<br><br>**ABC1 female**<br>Income codes 8 or 9; and if married and working f/t or 8-29 hrs/w, code 7; and if married and working f/t, code 6.<br><br>**C2DE male**<br>Income codes 7, 8 or 9; and HoH/CWE and married a⚫ wife is working f/t or p/t 8-2 hrs/w, code 6; or, if marrie⚫ and wife is working f/t, cod⚫<br><br>**C2DE female**<br>Income codes 7, 8 or 9; and married and working f/t or ⚫ 8-29 hrs/w, code 6; and if married and working f/t, code 5. | |
| **White**<br>Social Grade of HoH/CWE ABC1 | **Blue**<br>Social Grade of HoH/CWE C2DE | **White**<br>Social Grade of HoH/CWE ABC1 | **Blue**<br>Social Grade of HoH/CWE C2DE | **White**<br>Social Grade HoH/CWE ABC1 | **Blue**<br>Social Gra of HoH/C⚫ C2DE |
| DW | DB | PFW | PFB | FW+ | FB+ |

| ...age | Late Stage | |
|---|---|---|
| ...wife of HoH/CWE<br><br>...ults and children 0-15 or<br>...d informant is not a<br>...dent | All those not classified under Dependent, Pre-family<br>or Family Stage | |

| ...rse Off | **Better Off** | **Worse Off** |
|---|---|---|
| **...C1 male or famale**<br>...ormants not classified under<br>...C1 male or female better | **HoH/CWE or wife of HoH/CWE**<br>Age 65+; or aged 35-64 and household type adults only and informants has no children 16-20<br><br>if ABC1 male; income codes 7, 8 or 9; and if married and wife is working f/t or p/t 18-29 hrs/w, code 6; and if married and wife is working f/t, code 5.<br><br>if ABC 1 female; income codes 7, 8 or 9; and if married and working f/t or p/t 8-29 hrs/w, code 6; and if married and working f/t, code 5. | **HoH/CWE or wife of HoH/CWE**<br>Age 65+; or aged 35-64 and household type adults only and informant has no children 16-20.<br><br>if ABC male or female informants not classified under ABC 1 male or female Better off. |
| **...DE male or female**<br>...ormants not classified under<br>...DE male or female better | if C2DE male; income codes 6, 7, 8 or 9; and if married and wife is working f/t or p/t 8-29 hrs/w, code 5; and if married and wife is working f/t, code 5.<br><br>if C2DE female; income codes 6, 7, 8 or 9; and if married and working f/t or p/t 8-29 hrs/w, code 5; and if married and working f/t, code 4. | if C2DE male or female; informants not classified under C2DE male or female Better off. |
| | **Not HoH/CWE or not wife of HoH/CWE**<br>Age 35+<br><br>if ABC 1; SGA; or B if working f/t or p/t 8-29 hrs/w; or C 1 if working f/t.<br><br>if C2DE; working f/t. | **Not HoH/CWE or not wife of HoH/CWE**<br>Age 35+<br><br>if ABC 1; SGB and not working f/t or p/t 8-29 hrs/w; or C 1 and not working f/t.<br><br>if C2DE; not working f/t. |

| White<br>...cial Grade<br>...HoH/CWE<br>ABC 1 | Blue<br>Social Grade<br>of HoH/CWE<br>C2DE | White<br>Social Grade<br>of HoH/CWE<br>ABC 1 | Blue<br>Social Grade<br>of HoH/CWE<br>C2DE | White<br>Social Grade<br>of HoH/CWE<br>ABC 1 | Blue<br>Social Grade<br>of HoH/CWE<br>C2DE |
|---|---|---|---|---|---|
| **FW−** | **FB−** | **LW+** | **LB+** | **LW−** | **LB−** |

89

to provide additional classifications, which give newer insights into consumer behaviour. It helps to define the target markets by measuring consumers' actual behaviour in each product field of interest in total, and within SAGACITY groups. Demographic criteria have been combined, enabling informants to be placed into one of twelve groups. These groups are designed to be as homogeneous as possible, containing consumers at similar stages in their 'life cycle' and with similar disposable income and cultural characteristics. These different SAGAC-ITY groups are found to exhibit differing behaviour patterns over a wide range of markets. They reveal the actual nature of those markets, permitting the development of good target market definitions. The twelve groups also exhibit widely differing media usage habits and therefore offer a high level of discrimination between media.

The basic thesis of the SAGACITY groupings is that people acquire different aspirations and behaviour patterns as they go through their life cycle. The four main stages of the life cycle of adults aged over 15 are defined as follows (this example is taken from a specific survey year to show the relevant penetration figures):

1. *The dependent stage*: 16 per cent of all adults; describes consumers who are still living in their parents' household or studying full time if they live away from home.
2. *The pre-family stage*: 8 per cent of all adults; consists of adults under 35 years old who have already established their own households, but as yet have no children.
3. *The family stage*: 36 per cent of all adults; consists of all housewives and heads of household under 65, with one or more children in the household.
4. *The late stage*: includes all other adults whose children have already left home or who are 35 years or over and childless.

The other elements of the SAGACITY groupings are related to the income and occupational characteristics of the individual or couple forming the household. The income breakdown is applied only at the family stage and the late stage. This division by income rather than economic activity is particularly important at the late stage, as there is a significant minority of retired people who qualify for the 'better off' income grouping and who might be expected to exhibit similar consumption patterns to those who are still working. The last element used to form the twelve SAGACITY groups is the occupation of the head of the household. Individuals are grouped into non-manual (white collar) occupations (ABC1s) and manual (blue collar) occupations (C2DEs).

The following examples show the advantages of using SAGACITY in explaining the behaviour of a target market. A survey found that 20 per cent of all adults took a package holiday abroad, compared with 30 per cent in one SAGACITY group and 15 per cent in another. The index obtained from the analysis for the first SAGACITY group would be $30/20 \times 100 = 150$, and for the second $15/20 \times 100 = 75$. The market is greatly influenced by age and life cycle and divides into a young pre-family market and an older or late market. In the younger market the propensity for holiday taking is much higher amongst white collar occupations and this persists amongst the 'better off' white collar occupations even at the family stage. Amongst the younger blue collar occupations it is only those at the pre-family stage who have an above average index figure. At the late stage or older market the higher indices are amongst the 'better off', but the 'worse off' white collar group remains a reasonable target market for the package holiday companies.

Clearly, which groups to include in a target market definition, and their relative importance will depend on the type of package holiday offered. SAGACITY enables the user to make such a target market decision and then carry planning through to media selection.

Further use of SAGACITY shows that the readership of the 'quality' Sunday newspapers is primarily a 'better off' white collar phenomenon, but at equal strength at the pre-family and late stages. They also have a significant strength at the dependent stage but fall away heavily amongst the 'worse off' at the family and late stages. All blue collar groups have a low index, especially the 'worse off'. The single scale SAGACITY analysis therefore provides useful descriptions of markets for target market determination and good discrimination between media within those target markets. Its use may lead to different and more appropriate media decisions.

*ACORN (A Classification Of Residential Neighbourhoods)*
There is also another development in Europe for targeting customers by their life styles, which is known as ACORN (A Classification Of Residential Neighbourhoods). Developed initially in the UK, this system divides blocks of 150 addresses throughout the country into 39

**ACORN GROUPS**

| | | 1985 Population | % |
|---|---|---|---|
| A | AGRICULTURAL AREA | 1837585 | 3.4 |
| B | MODERN FAMILY HOUSING. HIGHER INCOMES | 9056851 | 16.8 |
| C | OLDER HOUSING OF INTERMEDIATE STATUS | 9519639 | 17.7 |
| D | OLDER TERRACED HOUSING | 2309097 | 4.3 |
| E | COUNCIL ESTATES – CATEGORY 1 | 7015875 | 13.0 |
| F | COUNCIL ESTATES – CATEGORY 2 | 4892746 | 9.1 |
| G | COUNCIL ESTATES – CATEGORY 3 | 3935124 | 7.3 |
| H | MIXED INNER METROPOLITAN AREAS | 2088892 | 3.9 |
| I | HIGH STATUS NON-FAMILY AREAS | 2265371 | 4.2 |
| J | AFFLUENT SUBURBAN HOUSING | 8531179 | 15.9 |
| K | BETTER-OFF RETIREMENT AREAS | 2048658 | 3.8 |

**ACORN TYPES**

| | | | |
|---|---|---|---|
| A1 | AGRICULTURAL VILLAGES | 1404704 | 2.6 |
| A2 | AREAS OF FARMS AND SMALLHOLDINGS | 432881 | 0.8 |
| B3 | POST-WAR FUNCTIONAL PRIVATE HOUSING | 2276963 | 4.2 |
| B4 | MODERN PRIVATE HOUSING. YOUNG FAMILIES | 1805955 | 3.4 |
| B5 | ESTABLISHED PRIVATE FAMILY HOUSING | 3173195 | 5.9 |
| B6 | NEW DETACHED HOUSES. YOUNG FAMILIES | 1475680 | 2.7 |
| B7 | MILITARY BASES | 325058 | 0.6 |
| C8 | MIXED OWNER-OCCUPIED AND COUNCIL ESTATES | 1877008 | 3.5 |
| C9 | SMALL TOWN CENTRES AND FLATS ABOVE SHOPS | 2185911 | 4.1 |
| C10 | VILLAGES WITH NON-FARM EMPLOYMENT | 2523830 | 4.7 |
| C11 | OLDER PRIVATE HOUSING. SKILLED WORKERS | 2932890 | 5.5 |
| D12 | UNMODERNIZED TERRACES. OLDER PEOPLE | 1349349 | 2.5 |
| D13 | OLDER TERRACES. LOWER INCOME FAMILIES | 752530 | 1.4 |
| D14 | TENEMENT FLATS LACKING AMENITIES | 207218 | 0.4 |
| E15 | COUNCIL ESTATES. WELL OFF OLDER WORKERS | 1879887 | 3.5 |
| E16 | RECENT COUNCIL ESTATES | 1460237 | 2.7 |
| E17 | BETTER COUNCIL ESTATES. YOUNGER WORKERS | 2642427 | 4.9 |
| E18 | SMALL COUNCIL HOUSES, OFTEN SCOTTISH | 1033324 | 1.9 |
| F19 | LOW RISE ESTATES IN INDUSTRIAL TOWNS | 2498587 | 4.6 |
| F20 | INTER-WAR COUNCIL ESTATES. OLDER PEOPLE | 1607711 | 3.0 |
| F21 | COUNCIL HOUSING. ELDERLY PEOPLE | 786448 | 1.5 |
| G22 | NEW COUNCIL ESTATES IN INNER CITIES | 1075117 | 2.0 |
| G23 | OVERSPILL ESTATES. HIGHER UNEMPLOYMENT | 1678631 | 3.1 |
| G24 | COUNCIL ESTATES WITH SOME OVERCROWDING | 839998 | 1.6 |
| G25 | COUNCIL ESTATES WITH MOST HARDSHIP | 341378 | 0.6 |
| H26 | MULTI-OCCUPIED OLDER HOUSING | 204279 | 0.4 |
| H27 | COSMOPOLITAN OWNER-OCCUPIED TERRACES | 577595 | 1.1 |
| H28 | MULTI-LET HOUSING IN COSMOPOLITAN AREAS | 388292 | 0.7 |
| H29 | BETTER-OFF COSMOPOLITAN AREAS | 918729 | 1.7 |
| I30 | HIGH STATUS NON-FAMILY AREAS | 1132770 | 2.1 |
| I31 | MULTI-LET BIG OLD HOUSES AND FLATS | 833500 | 1.5 |
| I32 | FURNISHED FLATS. MOSTLY SINGLE PEOPLE | 299101 | 0.6 |
| J33 | INTER-WAR SEMIS, WHITE COLLAR WORKERS | 3056752 | 5.7 |
| J34 | SPACIOUS INTER-WAR SEMIS, BIG GARDENS | 2671266 | 5.0 |
| J35 | VILLAGES WITH WEALTHY OLDER COMUTERS | 1560179 | 2.9 |
| J36 | DETACHED HOUSES, EXCLUSIVE SUBURBS | 1242982 | 2.3 |
| K37 | PRIVATE HOUSES, WELL-OFF OLDER PEOPLE | 1204778 | 2.2 |
| K38 | PRIVATE FLATS, OLDER SINGLE PEOPLE | 843880 | 1.6 |
| U39 | UNCLASSIFIED | 294080 | 0.5 |
| | | | |
| AREA TOTAL | | 53795097 | 100.0 |

**Figure 8.2** 1985 ACORN profile

different types of neighbourhoods, according to their demographic, housing and socio-economic characteristics. The system is based on an analysis of published statistics from the 1981 census.

The usefulness of this system is that it enables manufacturers and service providers to use their own customer address records, rather than rely on surveys to identify the types of area where they make the highest sales. They can also target their advertising expenditure, using only the media which are more effective in reaching their key ACORN type customers.

Companies that have used customer addresses to define ACORN types range from direct mail companies, financial organizations which hold addresses for every account holder, gas and electricity and TV companies which keep accounting information, retailers who operate credit card facilities, travel companies, motor appliance and furniture manufacturers who retain names and addresses for warranty or guarantee purposes, to charities and also political parties.

ACORN is used by insurance companies, building societies, credit operators and direct mail houses to identify the types of customer it is most profitable to service. They can identify from their own records which are the most loyal customers, in which parts of the country average order values are the highest, where bad debts are the lowest and where responsiveness to mailshots is the most effective.

ACORN analyses also show that building societies are better placed than banks to deliver financial services to areas of population growth. There are some 7,000 building society branches and 11,000 banks nation-wide, but the penetration of these varies widely across the country. In areas of high population growth the banks face stiff competition from building societies. For example, the fastest growing area of Britain, Milton Keynes, has nine building societies for every ten banks, which is above the national average. When 20,000 building society agents are added into the analysis of the UK, the picture is even clearer. Building societies have twice to four times as many outlets compared with the banks.

*Use of the ACORN system*

The classifications have proved to be very useful in determining the characteristics of different customer groups. For example, high status retirement areas are usually poor on expenditure per capita, but good

**93**

on loyalty. Modern council estates are good on mailing responsiveness, but bad on debt.

It is also possible to determine the different types of areas by assessing the age distribution. The analysis identifies:

- pre-family areas, of relatively high disposable income and low commitments
- young family areas, with a high level of mortgage, hire purchase and overdraft use.
- post family areas, with a high level of savings, low use of credit and high incomes
- retirement areas, with low income, but significant investment income.

ACORN is therefore widely used in market research, advertising and direct marketing. It is also of use to a sales manager for setting equitable sales targets for different sales territories. Until now the sales manager has had to take subjective decisions about the sales potential of various territories and has not had a definitive mechanism for setting sales quotas. Now, however, using ACORN and analysing customer addresses, the sales manager can set a sales target by each ACORN type. This extends to allowing for the population in each ACORN type within the sales territories. Quotas can now be set to relate to the potential for business in each area.

One other important application is 'site location', using information about ACORN profiles of each shopping centre to minimize the risk of opening an unprofitable shop. Retailers such as W H Smith and Boots are known to use ACORN to evaluate the product ranges that should be stocked at different stores in different parts of the country.

## Case study

The traditional research techniques available to determine the acceptability of the attributes of a product were seen earlier through the experience of Devro Ltd. The only information Devro Ltd had to use on the attitudes to its casings and how they compared with competitors was that fed to the marketing department from the salesmen. This information was mainly based on reports of what the sausage manufacturers were saying about the sales of the specific types of sausages. It was, therefore, essential to complement the existing research information by designing market research to evaluate consumers' attitudes not only towards the sausages and their different casings, but to the casings themselves.

The research used a specifically designed and structured questionnaire to incorporate the key characteristics of both sausages and casings, explored initially in group discussions. By putting together attribute statements about the sausage and its casing, the company was able to compare and identify preferences for sausages and their casings.

The research in this situation became a selling tool against competitive casing, one further element of the marketing mix, and helped to highlight the mistaken belief that consumers preferred animal gut, exploiting the statement 'a fine line between tradition and obsolescence'.

## Conclusion

Having identified the basic physical characteristics of the market, it is essential, in order to understand consumer behaviour, to discover the reasons for people's actions, what motivates and influences them:

- why do people act in certain ways?
- why do they hold certain opinions?
- why have they developed certain attitudes?

Marketing is concerned with change, adapting to change and creating change. Current and historic spending and savings patterns may provide a basis for market prediction. A healthy sales and profit record for a product, which has represented the best rationalized compromise available of customer needs and customer satisfaction, may be to little avail if a new product, nearer the customer's perception of the ideal, becomes available. Thus continuous analysis of consumer buying behaviour and decision making helps management to understand the consumer better, to market products the consumer wants, and to ensure that his total marketing effort is consumer-oriented.

**Checklist of questions for identifying and measuring consumer attitudes**

- Do we know how our customers and potential customers behave?
- Are their buying decisions changing?
- How do they make the decisions about the products they buy and the services they use? Are these decisions the same for buying our products?
- How are consumers motivated towards buying our products?
- How did the consumer first become aware of the product?
- What did the consumer believe were the main differences between our products and other products on the market? Which of the product attributes were the main ones to influence the consumer to buy our products?
- Have we classified our customers according to their lifestyles?

# 9

# Assessing and Improving the Sales Process

We have already seen, earlier in this book, the usefulness of research for successful marketing, proving that it is not just a marketing service tool within a company. Recent developments in the use of research techniques have also provided other benefits to the companies using them. One such benefit is the use of these techniques to research into marketing *methods*, as opposed to just investigating markets – in particular in evaluating selling, as sales managers realize how research can guide them to more productive sales activities.

Most marketing and sales managers find research aids their decision making. Analysis of research helps them to evaluate:

- where or why an action or decision should be made
- what type of action or decision is implied
- what is the result of implementing the 'action decision' and what are the implications for future decisions and future actions.

It is therefore not surprising that there is now a growth of the use of research for assessing the effectiveness of companies' marketing and sales methods in comparison with those of their competitors.

This type of research is being used in two ways:

1. to plan and manage the sales management activity in a company to ensure it has the desired 'synergy' with the overall marketing strategy.
2. to monitor, control and, if necessary, change the chosen sales strategy and sales plans.

## Research as an aid to sales management

Research is particularly useful if it provides guidance as to which sales methods are the most effective and which need to be allocated which resources. It is therefore important to design research to address the sales process specifically, rather than allowing it to be just one of the issues evaluated in a research project.

## Case study

Take, for example, the case of a clothing manufacturer who identified that its sales in one of its five sales areas had dramatically decreased in comparison to its previous performance. The company decided it had to research this problem to overcome this newly identified sales shortfall, and to help to plan the future sales strategy.

The questions the company wanted to answer were:

- Does the problem lie in the capabilities of our salesman in this one particular area?
- Does the problem lie in the way we sell our products in relation to our competitors' methods?
- Does the problem lie in our products, company image and total marketing approach in comparison with that of the competition?

The research solution appropriate for answering these questions concentrated on:

- evaluating the sales and marketing methods, personal selling, telephone selling, van sales, postal orders, etc, that each of the retailers used, as well as determining the effectiveness of these sales methods.
- determining how effective these methods were in supporting and communicating each supplier's products and company image.

(The checklist at the end of this chapter shows the type of questions that can be put to customers to assess the effectiveness of a company's sales activity.)

The research resulted in identifying that the sales problem in this one particular region related to the personality of the salesman in the area, compared with the salesmen from other companies, and company sales methods. Competitors had more effective systems for meeting retailers' changing needs – in this instance a telephone selling and weekly postal ordering system.

The benefit of completing research in this way is to be able to take a step back from the day-to-day tasks and determine how to improve the overall sales process. This type of project can be focused on the individual elements of the marketing mix as required; indeed, most market research carried out is completed for market definition, product development, advertising and sales promotion. Some companies, like the clothing company, are now spending their research budgets on establishing whether all elements of the marketing mix are achieving the 'synergy' they require for ensuring that the sales process is successful. These companies are therefore able to develop sales management systems which support and extend all aspects of marketing actions through advertising, promotion and selling.

The concept of determining whether the sales process is working in unison with the company's marketing activities overall has been taken a stage further by some companies in the financial services sector.

One of the most interesting aspects of marketing is the development and communication of the image of a company, as we have seen in an earlier chapter. The traditional approach to this was for companies to complete research to ensure that the image of the company is extended through effective advertising. Some financial services companies are now researching the success of communicating the company image not only through advertising, but also through selling, to ensure that both the required sales messages and the *methods* are supporting the overall communications strategy.

## Case study – research to aid sales planning

The basic principles of communication research – using it to plan effective communications and to monitor the effectiveness and results of its implementation – can be used in assessing the effectiveness of communications through the sales process. Take for example the case of an insurance company who took the decision to develop and improve its image in the market. The company planned some market research to determine whether its image was being communicated through its sales activities. This research was completed amongst three separate audiences as follows:

**99**

1. *Its customers and potential customers*
   This was to establish their perceptions of the company, as well as their attitudes to its image in comparison to those of its competitors. The research resulted in assessing the life insurance policy holders' perceptions of the company through all aspects of its communications – advertising, leaflets and mail shots, proposal forms, branch and head office services, etc.
2. *Intermediaries in the marketplace – life brokers, solicitors, bank managers, etc*
   This was to establish why these intermediaries selected the company and its services, rather than the services of its competitors. In addition, the research evaluated how the company image enhanced the overall sales processes, through all the company communications: contact with head office, agents and inspectors; promotional material sent to intermediaries; and information on new products, proposal forms, company information, etc.
3. *The insurer's own agents and salesforce*
   This was to determine whether those members of the sales team were communicating the right image and sales message effectively. In addition, this research was designed to determine whether their sales techniques and methods were 'synergistic' with the other aspects of the marketing mix, such as promotions and advertising.

The insurance company in this instance achieved the desired result. The benefit of this research was to enable them to plan and manage the sales activity, to ensure that it had 'synergy' with the overall marketing strategy. The company was therefore able to set its objectives in communicating its image and the sales techniques required for carrying it out. It then established criteria by which it could evaluate its image in the marketplace. In addition, it tested out the success of its selling with its customers, intermediaries in the market handling its services and its own salesforce.

## Case study – research to assess the effectiveness of sales methods

Another market also provides an example of how assessing the image of the company can help to improve the sales process. The map, atlas and travel guide book sector in the UK have formed a research syndicate.

**100**

One of the first surveys carried out asked a representative sample of retailers – multiples, independents, bookshops, wholesalers and confectioners, tobacconists and newsagents – for their views on the effectiveness of publishers' marketing of maps, atlases and travel guide books.

The survey found that a large proportion of the retailers said they believed publishers could help them to market and sell better to their customers. Other retailers said that 'more stands/display shelves were required and that there should be more in-store promotions'. In fact, in-store assistance appeared to be neglected by publishers. A further sample of the retailers said that there should be better marketing support through increased advertising and the supply of promotional materials.

The retailers were asked to rate the various marketing activities of all the publishers in the sector to give an overall assessment. They were then asked to rate the performance of selected publishers, such as the Automobile Association, Bartholomew, Collins, Estate Publications, Geographia, Michelin, Ordnance Survey, George Philip and RAC. Fourteen criteria were used, for example 'limited product range', 'good advertising' and 'lack of support through in-store promotions'.

As a result, the publishers were able to analyse and compare their own and their competitors' performance and to compare the retailers' perceptions of these against the retailers' feelings about the general performance in the sector.

Figure 9.1 shows how the individual publishers' images can be charted from the retailers' responses and compared against a competitor, and the sector average. Publisher A is one of the leading publishers in the sector, publisher B is a medium-sized company, and the third line shows the average performance of publishers in the market. The -100 to +100 rating above and below the table refers to the percentage of both negative and positive responses from the retailers in the survey to the criteria listed down the side of the table. In this analysis therefore it can be seen that publisher A's products are regarded as good by 70 per cent of the respondents and its product range as limited by 40 per cent of the retailers. Equally, compared with the other publishers, Publisher A is considered to have a limited product range and to lack forward-looking product development. Publisher B, however, compared with the other publishers is considered to provide support through

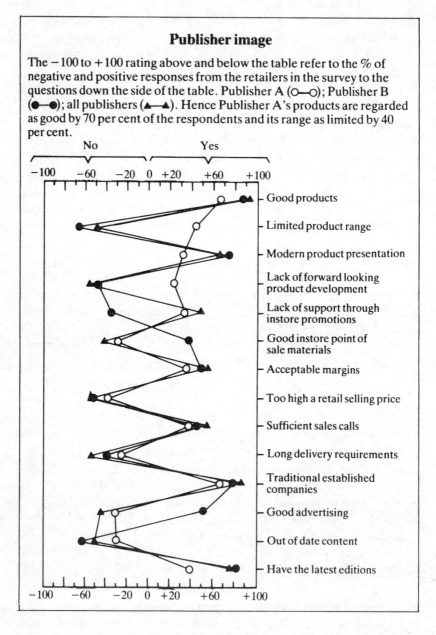

**Figure 9.1** Chart of publishers images

in-store promotions, to have good in-store point-of-sale materials and to have good advertising.

The findings of this research help in two ways. The publishers can check whether their marketing and communications strategies are effective amongst the retailer network, particularly in relation to the marketing methods of competitors. In addition, each can assess to what degree its salesforce is implementing its strategies and reflecting the required image. When weaknesses in sales and marketing methods are identified in relation to competition, the salesforce can be advised to improve on selected sales or marketing methods. Where there are strengths, the salesforce can be persuaded to continue to emphasize them and to diminish any counter threats from competition.

### Researching the sales process

Earlier, we looked at how research aids decision making and how some companies have used it to aid their sales decisions and sales activities. We also saw that a continuous flow of marketing research information is needed to manage this process. Research can help a company to improve the effectiveness of selling at the various stages of the sales process. There are six major areas where the sales manager can be helped:

- planning
- organization
- staffing
- training
- motivation of salesmen
- control of salesmen.

These are the key areas where decisions are taken every day on subjective and historical bases, but where data and information could guide the search for more effective methods. Of these areas the two which benefit the most from research are sales planning and sales organization. A third area to benefit is the general one of sales effectiveness.

## Research as an aid to sales planning

There are a number of ways in which research can be of assistance in sales planning. Having first established the objectives in the sales planning process, the next requirement is to consider what information will determine the most efficient means to achieve the objectives. Background market and customer knowledge is essential to the salesman because of the need to understand how the customers view their activities and, more importantly, their needs. Background knowledge also provides the salesman with an important attribute – confidence – and confidence communicates itself to customers. In general, the information that will be useful in sales planning depends on the selling problem. However, as a guideline the following questions should be answered:

- What are the characteristics of the market in which the selling is to be carried out?
- What are the trends in this market?
- What are the needs of the customers?
- How does competition serve this market?
- When do the customers normally buy the products/services?
- Where do they normally buy the products/services and how much will they pay for them?
- How much do they/will they buy and how will their needs change in the future?

Sources of information including colleagues, other customers, local and trade press, libraries, local authorities, directories, past records, etc, are very useful. However, unless these sources yield sufficient information on 'what' and 'why', 'effects' and 'causes', then it is probably going to be of little use to the salesman. Unless the sales plan is related to marketing intelligence information, market research data and market forecasts, provided by the marketing and research department, the sales planning process may not achieve the objectives it set out to obtain. Asking for and obtaining the right sort of information from the research department can ensure that the sales plan is realistic in relation to the market performance and the needs of the customers.

## Research as an aid to sales organization

The second area in which research can aid the sales manager is sales organization. Having established the market and its needs, the sales manager then has to determine how often customers should be contacted. This helps to ensure that there is a degree of productivity in the conducting of the sales activities. This means that the salesforce must be organized in relation to the needs of the market to which it is selling.

Salesforces are normally organized on the basis of four specific patterns. It is important to establish how research can determine the suitability of each in relation to the company which is doing the selling and the market which it serves. The four patterns are:

1. Allocation of sales areas by 'geographical areas'.
   What geographical split in our markets, customers, distributors, etc, is going to ensure that we achieve sales profitably?
2. Allocation of product types.
   What product specializations are there that require technical explanations and problems?
3. Allocation of customer types.
   What segmentation of our customer types will determine the type and ability of salesmen required?
4. Handling key accounts/house accounts.
   What resources are required to handle key accounts?

Marketing intelligence and market research can assist in the organization of a salesforce, provided that the sales manager calls on the research department to:

- provide existing data in answer to the above questions
- if necessary, re-analyse existing data to obtain the appropriate answers to these questions
- advise, set up, manage, run, analyse and report on specialist ad-hoc projects which will answer any outstanding questions.

Looking at the four areas again, marketing intelligence and research can provide data on:

1. *geographical splits*: in terms of location of customers, regional needs and tastes, even environmental differences and needs.
2. *product characteristics*: in terms of attitudes, needs and preferences for

different products in respect of different needs.

3. *customer types*: in terms of usage of products, socio-economic differences, and even cultural, political and habitual differences.
4. *key accounts*: in terms of the purchasing needs and purchasing methods in comparison with the rest of the company's customers.

Therefore, by using existing information, statistics on customers, their buying needs and habits, a company can formulate a sales organization to:

- segment customers into buying groups
- develop a sales organization to handle these groups
- organize sales staff to handle major customers
- organize sales staff to service customers
- introduce a degree of flexibility into the sales organization to meet changing demands in the market.

For example, over the last few years grocery and supermarket retailers have been analysing and re-analysing their market research data to achieve just this for their selling structures. More recently, financial services companies have recognized the importance of the customer information they have on their own computer databases. Thus, they have been matching internal data with external market research data and have been using it to assess their branch structures, staff requirements and new service offerings.

## Research as an aid to monitoring sales effectiveness

The third area in which research can aid the sales manager is in sales effectiveness. This mainly concerns the motivation of salesmen. Research in this area can be completed in two ways:

1. *Quantitative attitude research* into the relationship between different payment systems and sales results to see if commissions have the desired effects. There are a number of published annual surveys which provide this information.
2. *Qualitative attitude research*, identifying what incentives and disincentives the salesmen perceive within their jobs. There are situations in which companies have collected information on the salesforce's attitudes to their payments and their own results. Findings have

revealed misunderstandings in communication between marketing management, sales management and the salesmen.

The most popular method of completing such attitude research is through 'employee opinion polling', used to assess what motivates the salesforce in their jobs, as well as assess the morale and motivation of the salesforce.

## Case study – polling employee opinions

Take, for example, a chemicals company which, in re-allocating its resources, wanted to re-structure the salesforce and also the job specifications of its salesmen. The company had eight divisions serving different market sectors with a range of chemicals which could be used in a variety of applications. The objective of the company was to standardize the whole marketing and sales operation, including all elements of the marketing mix and the structure of the sales operation. Through an 'employee opinion poll' it found out how to ensure that following the company's rationalization the salesmen would be motivated to take on their newly defined roles.

The procedure the company adopted was as follows:

1. It commissioned an independent professional agency to conduct the poll.
2. Then, a representative sample of 100 salesmen in each of the eight divisions was selected for interview. Each interview was an in-depth attitude evaluation lasting one hour, covering all aspects of the subject.
3. The interviews were then analysed and the major issues highlighted.
4. Then, through a quantification study, a self-completion postal questionnaire was prepared for mailing to each of the salesmen in the company. Provision was made for evaluating overall opinions towards the major issues by listing a series of pre-coded questions. An example of this type of questionnaire is shown in Fig. 9.2.
5. The returned questionnaires were then analysed on the computer and an analysis prepared detailing:
   - the common strengths of the sales job as perceived by the salesmen themselves
   - specific strengths and weaknesses of the sales jobs in the various divisions

**107**

- the major issues concerning motivation and what actions the salesmen expect from sales management to improve it
- the major issues concerning the salesforce's morale and what actions the salesmen expect from sales management to improve it.

---

- What opinion do you have of the company's:
  - advertising and sales promotion?
  - products and new products being planned?
  - sales supplies and materials (order forms, etc)?
- What is your opinion of the company's:
  - territorial arrangements for sales areas?
  - sales quotas by areas and products?
  - benefit package for salesmen?
  - bonus schemes and incentives?
- What is your opinion of your sales manager in terms of:
  - the support he provides?
  - his knowledge of your problems?
  - his overall contact with you?
  - the motivation he provides you?
- What is your opinion of top management in terms of:
  - awareness of the problems the salesforce deal with?
  - overall contact with you?
  - support they provide?

---

**Figure 9.2** Questions for employee opinion polling

The results of this employee opinion poll in the chemicals company were that:

- the total remuneration package was revised because sales management had not appreciated the dissatisfaction caused by the various anomalies within the divisions
- a new incentive scheme was devised to increase morale and motivation.

Earlier in the book, we saw how companies have recognized, researched and understood the importance of customer opinions. In this chapter we have also seen how companies poll employees on attitudes to pay and conditions which could affect the level of service they provide. This has been taken a stage further by other companies as they have understood and compared the perceptions of staff towards their markets, the company and competitors, with those of the customers themselves.

## Case studies – assessing purchasing criteria

Take the case of three suppliers of industrial products who all needed to improve the margins achieved by their salesforces. Initially the senior management of all the companies believed the solution to their problem lay in negotiating an acceptable price. Research proved to the companies that price was not such a critical factor.

In the first company, a manufacturer of heavy machinery, management was convinced that their marketing strategy depended on effective pricing. As a result, sales training and field sales management resources were implemented with the sole aim of *changing these attitudes*. No one in the company tried to establish why they or their customers held such strong views on price.

The second company, suppliers of agricultural machinery, had had the same problem as the first company. However, their method of changing management's attitudes was to commission a study of customer buying attitudes. This was used to show the salesforce why its own views on pricing were wrong.

The third company, an industrial components supplier, approached the same problem by recognizing that if the opinions of customers and potential customers are fundamental to the sales effort, then so too are the views of the salesforce. It compared the salesmen's perceptions of their customers and potential customers with data collected from research amongst customers. Both groups, of course, have definite reasons for holding their opinions. The way to progress was not to 'persuade' the salesforce to change their opinions, but to rethink the approach of the company to the market. This involved the following:

- changing sales attitudes by learning more about the customers
- restructuring patterns of customer contact
- developing a total company approach to 'putting the customer first'.

**109**

One engineering and automotive components company identified and listed the perceptions of customer purchasing criteria from both customers and salesmen in order of importance. The rankings were as follows:

| Customer Ranking | Salesmen Ranking |
|---|---|
| Quality | Price |
| Reliable delivery | Quality |
| Rapid delivery | Technical advice/support |
| Rapid enquiry handling | Reliable delivery |
| Price | Product range |

This clearly shows that the salesmen were too price-conscious, and overrated the customers' requirements for technical support and comprehensive product range.

Discussions with the salesmen and customers pointed to reasons for the conflicting points of view. The customers accepted that, while a good product range and technical service were available from all major suppliers, significant differences existed on reaction times to product availability and on reliability. Prices were accepted as comparable and negotiation on price was used as a purchasing technique with suppliers only.

The salesmen were strongly influenced by the company's policy emphasizing product excellence and high levels of technical support capability. They had no direct contact with their order offices/delivery points, apart from problem chasing or checking up on orders from their sales areas. Much of their contact with customers was concerned with price negotiations. If either delivery or availability was mentioned, the query would be passed over to the relevant department.

So how could these differing perceptions be reconciled? The salesforce needed a better understanding of the company's approach to order-processing and delivery, as well as becoming far more aware of the complexity of the buying process amongst its customers. This in turn would encourage 'non-sales' staff to become more involved in improving service levels and also bring sales staff into contact with customers earlier in the sales process, in time to emphasize the high levels of product availability/delivery service.

Implementation involved questioning what the company's product offering was, followed by strategy development and the creation of a more 'open' organization, including setting up better structures for effective communication and programmes to improve staff knowledge levels and involvement. The returns from a more confident salesforce and service staff playing to their own strengths were considerable.

The implications of this type of approach are that management should not start with the premise that salesmen are automatically wrong in problem situations. For example, price is critical, although there are other, more important factors. The task is to explain why price is considered so important and what influences have contributed to it being so. The approach discussed earlier identifies how companies can differentiate between the techniques used by the salesforce and the other marketing techniques adopted for their marketing strategies. It facilitates the most cost-effective use of resources invested in the marketing mix and puts emphasis behind those factors that have priority in customers' buying decisions.

## Conclusion

Research, then, can help to improve the sales and selling process, as its practical application makes a positive contribution to management thinking and policy making.

The principles and techniques of research can be used to a greater extent in the future to evaluate, assess and improve the sales and marketing methods of any company. Specifically, research can be applied to help to improve the sales process by:

- aiding the overall marketing and sales planning activities, which highlight how the sales activity should be carried out;
- determining whether the communications process is supported, extended and enhanced by the abilities and the actions of the salesforce;
- establishing whether the sales process is being completed with the maximum efficiency and optimum effectiveness by the salesforce.

**Checklist of questions to customers for assessing the effectiveness of the sales activity**

- What opinion do you have of [the following companies] in terms of their:
    - products and product range, and new product development ability?
    - pricing, discounts and special price promotions?
    - packaging and new packaging development ability?
    - point-of-sales materials?
- What opinion do you have of [the following companies] in terms of their:
    - salesmen and their willingness to be of assistance to you?
    - sales office staff and their efficiency in dealing with your orders and queries?
    - telephone sales personnel and their effeciency?
- Thinking about the suppliers from whom you usually purchase your products, would you say that they have:
    - a modern or old-fashioned image?
    - ability to lead the market?
    - a good product range or limited product range?
    - forward product development?
    - acceptable margins?
    - good salesmen?
    - sufficient sales calls?
    - good delivery lead times?

# 10

# Developing a Marketing Information System

Before concluding how to use research effectively, it is important to highlight how information can be co-ordinated within a company. Market and marketing research injects a flow of data, information, and market or marketing intelligence. It is important for a company to use this data to ensure that its resources, methods, and actions match the needs of its customers.

It is therefore advantageous to develop a marketing information system to formalize the co-ordination process and make sure the data collected is used. In fact, research carried out amongst companies which use such marketing information systems has shown that not only have they developed a more co-ordinated approach, but also the marketing intelligence itself has become much more actionable.

**Why is it important to have a system?**

There is a danger when undertaking market research of collecting too much information and of not being able to use it effectively. A marketing information system enables the collection and use of data on which the company knows it can take positive actions. It also helps to define the following:

- What internal data is needed to assist the company to monitor its performance?
- What external data will aid the company to identify whether its

products and services are satisfying its customers and potential customers?

- Is the data required to solve a 'one-off' marketing problem?
- Is the data going to help to implement a 'short-term' action in the marketing plan?
- Is the data going to help develop and action the 'long-term' strategic plan?

In other words, would the provision of data supply sufficient information on the trends in the company's markets, the performance of the company within the marketplace, and the opinion of the customers or potential customers at whom it is targeting its products and services? And, if there is such data, is it being collected and analysed in such a way as to help the company know whether it is being successful or unsuccessful and whether it is taking the right or wrong decisions? A marketing information system will ensure that all of the 'vital' information will be collected, analysed, and referred to on a continuous basis.

## Setting up a marketing information system

As outlined in Chapter 2, it is important to prepare for a marketing information system carefully by developing a structured approach to what data is to be collected and how it should be used. The first decisions to be made are:

- How should it be set up?
- Who should be responsible for setting it up?
- How detailed should the system be?
- What type of information is needed – performance data, behaviour data, or attitude data?
- How much time will it take to set up?
- How much money should be allocated as a budget for setting up the system?
- How will it be run on a continuous basis and what will the ongoing costs be?

It is important to recognize from the outset that the most effective marketing information systems will be flexible, and capable of being developed and changed. Indeed, the users must also recognize that they need to:

**114**

- learn how to use them
- become skilled at managing the amount of data to put into and extract from them
- develop their knowledge to ensure that the information itself helps them to re-design and improve elements of the system
- update and improve the system over time.

## Elements of a marketing information system

Management in many companies in Europe admit that they often take decisions without using information, particularly without being aware of customers' 'true' needs and reactions to their actions. Certain elements of a successful information system can help to change the negative attitudes of management towards the use of data.

*Internal operating data*
The data generated by a company itself is a vital part of the information system. This 'internal operating data' provides key intelligence and should include:

- sales trends
- price information
- marketing support data
- distribution level data
- stock level data
- production targets
- quality control
- waste management
- energy usage
- repair and maintenance
- budgets.

However, companies frequently generate monthly analyses as general computer printouts, yet fail to analyse the data effectively. The row of figures is studied in isolation, with no attempt to interpret their meaning by comparing figures or drawing out trends. Or it can be that a company bases its decisions on this data alone, without reference to the external environment or even the opinions of its customers.

**115**

*External data*

In Chapter 3 we saw the importance of 'mapping' a market in the process of market analysis. Each company needs to define its key sources of information to assess the size of its markets, the shape of these markets, and the trends within these markets. In Chapters 4–9 we looked at different aspects of information that can be collected from the marketplace. This includes:

- defining consumers' needs for products and services
- identifying which new products and services can be developed
- monitoring products' sales and performance in the market
- assessing ways in which to communicate with customers and potential customers
- identifying the success of these communications
- understanding consumer behaviour and lifestyles
- assessing the effectiveness of the sales process.

If a company collects this data it needs to be able to decide how to use and interpret it. It also needs to identify which facts within the mass of this information are the 'key determinants' which should be regularly referred to and monitored.

Management's aim should therefore be to have a marketing information system which enables it to identify regularly the sales levels for all products in all its chosen markets, the levels of stock within its distribution network, and its current levels of output. This needs to be analysed in conjunction with trend data, market share analyses, and information on the sales success and profitability of each of the products. The system which will make this information more coherent and co-ordinated can be developed into a database 'tailor made' to the company and its needs.

## Case study – setting up the marketing information system

Take, for example, a company in the building products sector. Established over 100 years ago, it supplies products in the industrial sector to construction, civil engineering companies, and the utilities, and DIY products in the retail sector to builders merchants, plumbers merchants, DIY shops, and superstores. The company's headquarters are in the UK, with manufacturing operations in the USA, Canada,

**116**

South Africa, Australia, and New Zealand.

The management of the company relied on little data to take its decisions. Every month the Board would call a meeting of the key sales management to discuss progress. During these meetings the following key activities were carried out:

- Each manager would read through his report (submitted a fortnight before the meeting) which listed the progress of each of the sales activities or projects.
- The finance director would read out the monthly sales analysis, providing a breakdown of sales by each company in the group, a comparison with sales for the same month in the previous years, and a comparison with the sales target for the month. He would also comment on the profitability of the company in the past month.
- Marketing services would read out the number of advertisements placed in the last month, the number of PR releases, whether it had bought promotional items, etc.
- Production would account for the hours worked, quality control performance, and list all maintenance and repair activities in the last month.

No reference was made to any external or market data and indeed the marketing services department contained no published information and there was no library of periodicals and journals in the company.

It was clear that the company needed to think more strategically, become analytical in its approach to decision-making, and take a more creative and innovative approach to marketing.

The company decided to take advantage of the Department of Trade and Industry's Marketing Initiative and asked a marketing consultancy to set up a project to develop a strategic marketing plan. A full marketing audit was completed, an analysis of the company's strengths, weaknesses, opportunities and threats carried out, a mission statement created, and marketing strategies agreed. The key focuses of the plan were: to understand what customers' attitudes were; to identify what trends existed in the different markets in which the company operated; and to develop some ideas which needed to be tested out through market research.

The result was the development of a marketing information system which provided data and intelligence over and above the facts collected at the monthly management meeting. The important point that emerged was that the different companies within the group needed their own system and their own sources of information. They were as follows:

1. *International subsidiaries*

   Using the resources of the Export Market Research scheme, an annual survey of the global market was commissioned from an international research company based in the USA. The report on the study provided data on the size, shape, and nature of the market in which the company operated. Continued subscription to the annual data report would in time also provide trends in the market. In a year or two there was a further plan to commission *ad hoc* research to explore some of the key issues emerging from the trends, in selected countries in which the subsidiaries operate.

2. *The UK industrial and construction sector*

   The marketing audit revealed that the company believed that this sector was in decline because of substitute products being used more widely. Desk research failed to provide any published data to corroborate this. An *ad hoc* survey was then set up amongst both current and potential customers to establish their needs for the products and their expectations of their use for them in the future. The survey revealed that in fact the company was failing to penetrate the market effectively. A high proportion of the target customers said that they did not know the full range of the company's products. Consequently, it was felt to be important to set up this survey annually to monitor whether improved sales and marketing tactics increased penetration of the market and to assess whether customers' attitudes towards the product range improved.

3. *The UK DIY and retail sector for building products*

   The marketing audit of the retail company in the group showed that 30 years ago the product range led its segment of the market. Lack of marketing support and investment in new product development and packaging, as well as lack of innovative communications, had caused the popularity and sales of the product range to diminish.

   Desk research revealed a wealth of published reports on the state of the market, identifying stagnation in the growth of the DIY sector. This also provided information on the role of the multiple retailers, identifying that they were asking for more favourable terms and conditions while introducing other ranges of domestic and household products to uphold profitability in an increasingly competitive market. Consequently, the company found it was competing for shelf space at a time when the trade were questioning whether their customers wanted to purchase the products.

Three actions were taken to improve the intelligence in the company on the DIY and retail sector.

The first was the development of an information unit based on the collection of market and product information from published reports and surveys, trade and consumer journals, and the national and local press. A press cuttings service was developed to circulate key articles to all levels of management (including to overseas subsidiaries) which gave them ongoing competitive and market data.

The second action was to set up an annual *ad hoc* research project amongst householders to establish the extent to which they complete DIY tasks. Three hundred 15-minute telephone interviews were completed at random across the UK, in the evenings and at weekends. The results of these gave the company the following data:

- a basic profile of the DIY enthusiast and the consumer awareness (and in most cases unawareness) of the company's own range of products.
- a listing of all the DIY tasks completed and those they would be prepared to complete, some of which related to current products in the company's range.
- a full analysis of newspapers read, amount of TV watched and radio listened to, which assisted in identifying the appropriate media to use for advertising.

The third task was to set up an annual *ad hoc* research project amongst the trade, to establish the degree to which the company was supporting the trade in its sales and marketing compared with competition. Four hundred personal interviews were carried out with the buyer in multiple outlets, DIY shops, plumbers merchants, builders merchants, wholesalers and buying societies. The results of these gave the company the following data:

- an analysis of how well the company was supporting the trade in

**119**

terms of marketing, communications and sales personnel.

- an identification of where penetration in the distribution network was weak.
- an assessment of how the trade believed the marketing of the company's products could be improved, apart from negotiating the best discount and terms and conditions.

*Conclusion*

The company now has in place a new system, a new flow of information and new facts on which to take decisions. The most effective way of utilizing the new data was to take it to the monthly management meetings and to add it to the internal data which was used to broaden the ideas and decisions management needed to take.

## Using a marketing information system

The essence of a marketing information system is to have at hand a computer analysis which provides:

- from internal data: weekly or monthly sales information for all products in the different parts of the company, production levels, and capacity utilization.
- from external data: information on consumer attitudes, advertising levels and changes in competitive sales and marketing methods.

Using a system effectively depends on a number of factors:

- understanding what a database can provide.
- recognizing that data must not be 'voluminous' but actionable.
- ensuring it is continuously developed and updated.
- recognizing that it needs developing over a period of time (maybe 2–3 years) before the company can conclude it has an effective and actionable system.

Every company needs to customize the computer material that it requires to set up a regular monitoring system. Figure 10.1 shows the type of internal information originally used by the company in the case study. Each month all it did was to look at the sheet shown, without using it in any other way. It was not plotted graphically to identify

**120**

| Retail sales | Current month | | | | | | | | | | | | Year to date | | | | | | | | | | | | |
|---|---|---|---|---|---|---|---|---|---|---|---|---|---|---|---|---|---|---|---|---|---|---|---|---|---|
| | Sales | | Budget | | Sales by outlet type | | | | | | | | Sales | | Budget | | Sales by outlet type | | | | | | | |
| Product group A | Value | Quantity | Value | Quantity | M | I | BM | PM | W | BS | Other | | Value | Quantity | Value | Quantity | M | I | BM | PM | W | BS | Other |
| *Sizes*  1 metre | | | | | | | | | | | | | | | | | | | | | | | | |
| 2 metres | | | | | | | | | | | | | | | | | | | | | | | | |
| 4 metres | | | | | | | | | | | | | | | | | | | | | | | | |
| 6 metres | | | | | | | | | | | | | | | | | | | | | | | | |
| **Product group B** | | | | | | | | | | | | | | | | | | | | | | | | |
| *Sizes*  1 metre | | | | | | | | | | | | | | | | | | | | | | | | |
| 2 metres | | | | | | | | | | | | | | | | | | | | | | | | |
| 4 metres | | | | | | | | | | | | | | | | | | | | | | | | |
| 6 metres | | | | | | | | | | | | | | | | | | | | | | | | |
| **Total** | | | | | | | | | | | | | | | | | | | | | | | | |

**Figure 10.1** Retail sales computer analysis

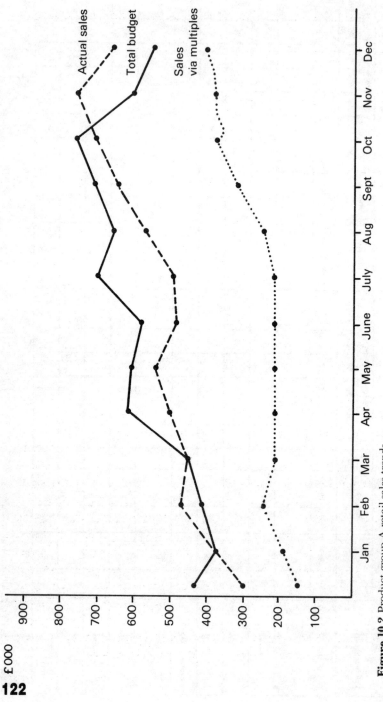

**Figure 10.2** Product group A retail sales trends .

**Table 10.1** Internal information used before a marketing information system was implemented

| | Total | Age | | | Social class | | | |
| --- | --- | --- | --- | --- | --- | --- | --- | --- |
| | | *18–24* | *25–34* | *35+* | *AB* | *$C_1$* | *$C_2$* | *DE* |
| **Mending gutters** | | | | | | | | |
| Yes | 35 | 60 | 42 | 35 | 40 | 55 | 58 | 35 |
| No | 65 | 40 | 58 | 65 | 60 | 45 | 42 | 65 |
| **Repairing cracked windows** | | | | | | | | |
| Yes | 42 | 55 | 58 | 35 | 41 | 56 | 59 | 32 |
| No | 58 | 45 | 42 | 65 | 59 | 44 | 41 | 68 |
| **Readership of papers** | | | | | | | | |
| *Sun* | 58 | 60 | 40 | 20 | 40 | 55 | 58 | 35 |
| *Daily Mirror* | 52 | 62 | 45 | 18 | 25 | 60 | 60 | 45 |
| *Daily Express* | 38 | 45 | 55 | 55 | 58 | 45 | 42 | 30 |
| *Daily Telegraph* | 28 | 42 | 58 | 55 | 60 | 45 | 30 | 25 |

trends, nor was it analysed for the best performing product range or product size within the range. Figure 10.2 shows the type of analysis that might have been more useful for management meetings and decision-making for monitoring sales via multiples.

Equally, assessing external data over a long period will help to follow the trends in the market and the needs and attitudes of customers. Table 10.1 shows an extract from the DIY company's consumer household survey carried out through telephone interviews. The data was collected for the company to identify users of its gutter repair and cracked window products. It was particularly important to identify the profile of this market and assess which newspapers are read to decide on the budget allocation for daily newspaper advertising. In this instance, gutters are mended by the 18–24 age group and the $C_1$ and $C_2$ social classes. The 18–24 age group and $C_1$ and $C_2$ social classes also read the *Sun* and *Daily Mirror*. Thus the advertising in these papers needed to be young and modern to attract the high-spending, young social class. The problem with this data is that it is a 'snapshot'; it needs to be collected continuously to ensure that sales, marketing and communications are targeted at the current market and potential customers.

**123**

## Conclusion

Marketing as a management tool is the means of ensuring that a company's goods and servics are supplied to its customers effectively. Marketing information and research is the means by which data is collected to identify the market and customer needs.

Developing a marketing information system helps a company to:

- decide on its requirements for research and information
- assess what internal management systems, external data sources, and data-based computer systems are required
- decide what *ad hoc* and continous data is needed, and what statistical, attitudinal, and motivational data will assist management to understand the market in which it operates, as well as the success of its marketing.

The marketing information system centralizes all the data a company needs to operate effectively. Long-term use of the system allows management to discriminate between good information and 'data for interest sake only'. Information systems therefore make a very important contribution to the effective use of market research.

## Checklist

- From where can we collect internal data?
- Who will be responsible for collecting it, updating it, and analysing it?
- What regular data will help us to monitor our markets and sales and marketing methods?
- What skills do we need to develop to run and use the system effectively?
- What internal data do we have that needs to be used from the system regularly?
- What external data is needed to complement the internal information?
- How should the system print out the information to produce an actionable and intelligible format?
- How can it be plotted graphically?

**124**

- What classifications are needed to distinguish the trends in our different customer types?
- What new system developments will be required as the company increases its activities?
- How can the data be improved and developed to help us take the right decisions?

# 11

# The Effective Use of Market Research

We have seen throughout this book that market research is an essential tool in the marketing planning process and plays a vital part in the business decision-making process. Its application is effective in all industrial, commercial and consumer markets. More importantly, the results that can be achieved from the market research process are the real objective of the business plan. They are also the most significant element of the marketing mix to influence business decisions.

Therefore, for marketing actions to be taken after the research is completed, it is vital to ensure that, as part of the outcome of the market research, the user is presented with recognizable decision options. As discussed in Chapter 3, the user should also have the confidence in the market research, the market research company and the company's personnel, to make the decisions with certainty and with the backing of the correct detailed analysis of the market.

This confidence must come in the very initial stages of recognizing the need to use market research. It will also come from the initial choice of the market research company, the interaction with its executives and the definition of the marketing problem to be tackled. Therefore, the choice of the market research company becomes the first major decision to be taken before the research can commence.

## Choosing the research company

The first set of key points to consider is as follows:

- Satisfy yourself that the company is competent to understand your market and any technical details, if necessary. Look for details of work carried out in similar fields and that it has been carried out regularly, not as a 'one-off' project.
- Establish that your marketing problem and your company are important to the research executive *and* the key decision-makers in the organization.
- Ensure that you are aware of who will manage the project and who will carry out the work.
- Try to establish that long-term continuity of personnel can be achieved with the executives involved.
- Question whether sub-contractors such as additional interviewers or special computer services are to be employed. If so, identify their role and the level of briefing they will obtain. Check for confidentiality and conflict of interests with the sub-contractor, as well as the project co-ordinator.
- If quick action is vital, check that the correct forms of communication are available, eg telex, fax, etc.
- The research company's membership of professional associations, such as the Market Research Society and the Industrial Market Research Association, and the Institute of Marketing, also provides added assurances through the relevant Codes of Conduct.

## Carrying out the research

A major factor affecting the choice of company to use for the project is the confidence that the user will have in the *results* of the research. This really comes back to the simple question of the validity of the data in the proposed exercise and whether it will remain valid in the long term.

Taking each type of research technique involved, ask the following questions:

### Desk Research

- Is the initial database a reliable source? Will it be published frequently and generally without amendments (unless the amendments are fully recorded)? Is any historical data available?
- Is too much reliance to be placed on estimates from manufacturers

or distributors in the industry, as opposed to systematic analysis of statistics?

- Is the factual data to be separated from estimated data and the work analysed for variability of the estimated data?
- Are all sources of data to be recorded for future work?
- Will the research give a picture of the whole market, and be properly analysed into accurate market sectors?

## Qualitative Surveys

- Have enough groups been chosen to cover all the demographic profiles such as age, sex, and regional differences?
- Is it important to explore competitive products or services at this stage?
- Is it possible to attend more than one interview session early in the research, to check cross-interpretations of responses?

## Quantitative Surveys

- Is the market population profile known? Can the sample for the research be related to the population?
- Are the rating scale points in the questionnaire between 'agree' and 'disagree' statements set to measure differentials?
- Does the sample of informants to be interviewed include the non-buyer or the non-user of our products or services?
- Does the sample of informants to be interviewed include the user and not the buyer of our products or services?
- Has room been left in the questionnaire to explore alternative uses of the products or services?
- Is there a series of questions to explore future product developments?
- Is it possible to attend at least one briefing and research survey location, to check progress and that the objectives are being achieved by the field research team?

## Briefing the research company

Before looking at some particular examples of how research became actionable for their users, we shall consider the actual briefing of the market research company. It is at this stage, if the correct preparation work is carried out, that the company can ensure that the most actionable results will be produced.

Obviously, most research is commissioned because a marketing problem has been identified. Research can be used for new product development, and market testing, but much of it is used to understand how to approach a market. Good marketeers wanting to use their research effectively for decision making will ensure that the research brief and the market research project include all elements of the marketing problem, and are not merely kept within the narrow confines of the 'expected result' of the project. It is therefore important to have good liaison between client and research company to discuss the proposed marketing methods. This will ensure that the results will achieve much more than just being a set of sterile data sheets: they will indicate which of the sales and marketing methods are the most and the least acceptable in the marketing situation being researched.

It is important to include in the brief:

- the effects of competitors' products or services.
- the behaviour of non-buyers or non-users.
- the traditional, current and future uses of the product or service.
- the benefits of the product or service to all consumers in the commercial chain.
- sufficient scope within the context of the research to examine issues beyond the particular marketing activity, giving opportunities in the questionnaire to explore future marketing planning.

It is particularly vital to consider this last aspect in the briefing. It not only provides the basis for any future marketing activities, but forms the basic elements in a strategic market research activity. As has been stressed throughout this book, market research is not a 'one-off' exercise, set down as a set of tabular results. It is an activity at the heart of marketing planning and decision making and it is only through a series of planned, co-ordinated and linked research activities that a company has the basis from which to achieve actionable results leading to success in the marketplace. The key point here is always to include questions designed to elicit information necessary for *moving on to the next stage of the marketing activity*. This will help a company to look beyond the current task and into the future role of its products or services. An ongoing

**130**

programme of market research is therefore necessary, to ensure that all the answers to today's problems are obtained; some may think that this merely gives full employment to the research company for an indefinite period of time, but in reality it is a recommendation based on a wish to achieve today what will lead towards tomorrow's successes.

Marketing people are looking towards 'tomorrow's markets' and an integrated market research programme provides the stepping stones by which to travel there. For market research to become actionable in terms of total business planning, it must be planned fully and carefully for today and tomorrow.

## Completion of the research

Once the research has been completed, it is vital that the data are available in a form which will assist the decision-making process. The following points are therefore worthy of consideration.

- Ask for an interim report before agreeing the final report on the research, checking that all the cross-analyses are available.
- Discuss this interim report with the research company, establishing the results of the research and what decision-making data are available. The final report should then highlight all the actions that are possible from the findings.
- Ensure that at least one copy of *all* data is available, even if it does not appear in the report. It may be required for future work.
- A presentation to the project management team should cover:
  the marketing problem tackled by the research
  the method of research (in outline only)
  the main analytical data produced
  how the results of the research can influence marketing and sales decisions and, in time, the overall business.

## Case studies

Let us now look at a number of case studies which will assist in showing how:

1. market research was used to achieve significant marketing success.

2. market research was used to strengthen a company's advantage over competitors.
3. market research did not provide the results expected by the company, causing management to analyse the situation further and take new decisions.
4. results were used to re-orientate the company's marketing and sales planning.

### Case study – using results to influence the market successfully

The first company is involved in supplying artificial flavourings to major food producers. It had as its main competitor a company marketing 'natural flavourings'. In reality, both products were derived from natural raw materials, with the lead company only reprocessing the product to allow ease of use and greater consistency for its customers' processes. As a result it had the major part of the market. However, the competitor tried to emphasize its products' 'natural state', despite the fact that productivity gains obtained from the processed product were advantageous to the user and no apparent difference could be detected in the final end product so far as the producer was concerned.

The lead company's American counterpart was experiencing major marketing problems with a similar situation in its home market. Again, there was an alternative 'natural product' produced by a company who successfully used this 'natural' profile. As a result of exchange rate changes, the prospect of this American product being available at a competitive price in the UK, marketed according to this natural profile, became a possibility.

The UK lead company, recognizing the impending competition from the US product and the possible resurgence of its domestic competition, questioned how this would affect their market. It therefore briefed a market research consultancy to analyse the situation and recommend what activities should be undertaken to protect its markets. It became clear that no one knew what the real effect of the flavouring was on the product, beyond the normal technical use. The research consultancy suggested a programme of market research to examine any differences in the three flavourings within the product, in the opinions of the user and the consumer but not the manufacturer.

Conventional consumer quantitative research through hall testing was carried out with all three variants. The expected outcome of the research was that no difference would be perceived by the consumer and that 'naturalness' would not be an issue. In fact, the research, although confirming this latter issue, did not give an even result between the variants, but suggested that the end product with the lead company's flavouring gave an added quality to the product.

The lead company was now in a very strong position to action these results in an aggressive marketing campaign, designed to show its customers that their consumers could differentiate between flavourings and that its product was preferred. The outcome of the research gave a leading edge to the UK company and this was subsequently marketed very efficiently to its benefit.

It is also worth commenting that had the market research findings been negative to the UK company, it would nevertheless have been ready to establish a technical research and development programme to overcome any product deficiencies. Clearly, the market research was the linchpin of the company's decision-making process and the results led to successful marketing activity.

In this situation, the company had recognized a marketing problem, had explored the extent of the problem through market research and, when the results were obtained, used them to influence its market significantly.

## Case study – assessing competitive advantages

The second case study involves the company Devro Ltd, which has been discussed in previous chapters. In this instance the company's extensive technical research and development facilities had been working on a project to improve the company's product performance with its customers, as a result of feedback from the marketing department. This feedback indicated that the manufacturing rates of sausage production were increasing rapidly as a result of improved machine technology, and the company's casing products would have to cope with this increased demand. A battery of scientific tests had shown that a new product had a significantly improved operating strength, with no detrimental effect on the eating properties of the sausage product. The question therefore became one of how to use this to the best marketing advantage.

The company had previously used market research to communicate to customers that its casing products gave significantly better eating characteristics with sausages than other competitive casing products. We saw in the previous chapters the type of rating statements that were used to determine preferences for the products. The company decided to use the same technique again to establish the profile of the consumer of this new product.

A series of consumer tasting sessions was carried out using hall tests throughout the UK with sausages in different casing products. Once again, use was made of the same consumer criteria confirmed in previous market research to establish differences particularly in taste, bite, and chewiness for each casing product. Both competitors' and the company's own existing and proposed new products were tested in the research. As was expected from the results of the scientific data, the consumer tests showed no significant difference in eating characteristics between the existing and new Devro Ltd products. The lead over the competitive products was maintained.

Clearly, Devro Ltd was now in a position to use this market research to its competitive advantage. A series of presentations was made to major and potential new customers, highlighting the improved operational qualities of the product, designed to increase user's productivity, without being detrimental to the consumers' perception of the final product. This activity allowed Devro Ltd to strengthen its position in its existing markets, while establishing its credibility with users of other casing products.

Once again, market research was able to help Devro Ltd make the initial decision to launch the new improved product and use the results of the research competitively.

## Case study – reappraising the results

The third case study involves a packaging company whose main product base was the manufacture of high quality printed cartons and boxes. The company had recently invested in the most modern production plant, capable of producing superior quality products at lower costs and with a reduced turn-around compared to their competitors. Once the plant was in operation, it was realized that the necessary production volumes were not being achieved from the sales orders to make the plant viable. So the company decided to carry out market research with its existing and potential customers, to establish its market profile before deciding how to develop a strategy to obtain an increase in market share.

In-depth interviews were carried out with the major purchasers in the market to establish their attitudes towards the leading suppliers of packaging in terms of price, delivery, quality and general company image. Each individual supplier was rated in these terms against the other suppliers. The original packaging company had believed that the results would show the company to be amongst the leaders in quality and delivery performance, but average in terms of price.

The market research results, however, were not as expected. In fact, the results suggested that the company was bottom of the league on all factors except quality. In addition, it showed that the company had an overall image of being a 'slow reacting company', only to be used for special work not required quickly and where price was not important.

These results obviously surprised the company and did not provide the answer to how to increase the volume throughput and the commercial viability of the production plant. As the results were being considered by management, certain more positive features became apparent.

First, they realized that the quality image was favourable and that it was a major reason why the company had the image of being a specialist work supplier. Secondly, the comments on poor delivery had been those associated with the company before its investment programme, and the buyers interviewed were not necessarily aware of the new plant and production facilities. Lastly, the perception of specialist work did not link with pricing, which was considered unimportant in this area.

Clearly the company's initial marketing strategy of being a high volume, low cost and quality producer was at variance with the market's image. It was also apparent from the results that a more significant market niche was available. Since its image was specialist, and once the message of increased volume with rapid delivery could be passed into the market, it would be possible for the company to increase its market share. More importantly, as this type of work was not price sensitive, higher profits could be made without direct comparison to competitive suppliers.

Here we have seen that the expected results of the market research were not obtained and the company's initial marketing approach appeared to be failing. As a result of the market research, intuitive analysis of the outcome showed that a definite marketing approach was possible which could provide greater success than had initially been targeted in the marketing plan. The market research gave the company much more actionable results than had been thought possible in the initial marketing planning.

## Case study – reorganizing sales and marketing planning

Our last case concerns a distributor of industrial consumable products, whose pricing policy had limited its operation to a sector of user companies who were not sensitive to price. Although acceptable profit levels were achieved in this market sector, little growth was possible. The company was also aware that this sector did not represent the largest share of the market and that growth could also be gained if it moved into other sectors. Clearly, the company had to establish the potential of the remaining market and decide what marketing strategy was appropriate to gain entry.

The initial phase of market research involved conventional desk research to confirm the number of UK establishments who were users of the company's products. In this case, use was made of local government rating statistics, which give a satisfactory breakdown of outlets by type, eg industrial, commercial, and retail, and of the establishments which were potential users of the company's products.

The second stage of the research involved a survey of users to establish annual expenditure on the products across each outlet type. This was carried out over an acceptable representative sample of users and the results cross-referenced against government published statistics on population.

Subsequently, the company was able to match both sets of data and confirm the market size in total, and by sector. They found that they operated in 25 per cent of the total market sector, yet they had a 10 per cent market share overall. In addition, the major user market represented 20 per cent of the market and the company was not represented in that sector in any way. The results also showed that the company was a major supplier to the market as a whole and no other supplier had more than 5–7 per cent of the market (it was a multi-supplier market of over fifty companies).

Clearly, the company would achieve its growth targets by entry into the major user market. The key question was how this was to be achieved. It was decided to commission a market research consultancy to carry out in-depth interviews with their main competitors in the major user market, to establish their attitudes to the market and their marketing approach towards the buyers of the consumable products concerned. This project was commissioned in conjunction with a major UK manufacturer, who was concerned by the high level of imported products used in this sector. As this company always operated through distributors, it wished to find a way of improving its own product presentation to the market.

The results of the research suggested that price was perceived as the dominant issue by the suppliers. They also believed that the customer was generally unconcerned with the products' origins, provided quality was maintained. Although lower margins were achieved by the nature of the order volume, acceptable profits could also be maintained.

The company was now in a position to work with the major supplier and establish a marketing strategy for both of them to achieve market penetration. Firstly, the manufacturer, by increasing volume through-put, was able to reduce unit costs, which could be used to allow extra discounts to the supplier company. This discount was used in an aggressive pricing policy by the supplier company to achieve market share in the major user sector.

Secondly, as the products involved were already supplied to the company's existing market sector, a lower buying cost was obtained and hence higher profit margins were achieved in this mature market sector by the company.

To summarize, the results of two separate stages of market research were combined to establish a market profile, and a marketing strategy to allow the company to break out of the strait-jacket of one market sector and operate in other sectors successfully.

The results of the research achieved two goals:

1. an increase in market share in new market sectors, and
2. increased profit margins on existing operations.

The first goal had been part of the initial market planning, the second a spin-off from the marketing strategy employed as a direct result of the market research.

These case studies show that market research can provide more than just data on the numbers in a market and the proportion that like or dislike a product, an advert or a marketing idea. It can provide companies with results which management can use directly to achieve their marketing objectives, by indicating what sales and marketing methods should be tried and tested.

Each of the companies discussed was competing effectively in its own market even before it carried out market research. However, they recognized that they needed to obtain a fuller picture of the market in order to achieve further development and success. They worked with a marketing consultancy company to define their marketing problem clearly and not only research this marketing problem, but put the research findings into the context of the market as a whole.

The company described in the first case study recognized aggressive activity by a competitor and the need to understand fully the influence of the 'end-user' on the market. Once the parameters of this influence were understood and their criteria for purchase clarified, the company was in a better position to make effective use of the market research. In this situation the company decided to neutralize the competitor's activity and re-establish its own market position and market share.

Devro Ltd used the 'end-user' market research internally to co-ordinate both scientific and product development testing with the communications used by the salesforce when developing customer confidence in the benefits of introducing new products. In addition, the results of the research convinced its management that a continuous research programme was required to provide vital information on and monitoring of market trends on which to base future sales and marketing decisions. This programme would therefore provide actionable results on an ongoing basis.

The packaging company case study provides a useful example of a company that had taken a decision on what they wanted from market research, but had to face up to the findings which presented them with new and important implications. As the company and its marketing

**138**

consultancy company had structured the research project to cover the entire market and the marketing issues affecting the company, they identified areas in which other sales and marketing methods needed to be improved and developed. Adjustments to the subsequent sales and marketing methods brought about significant changes. Careful interpretation of the research results provided the company with the success it had wanted, but in a way it had not expected.

The final example of the industrial distributor used the analysis of the market provided by the market research to increase not only market share but also the profitability of the company as a whole. Its immediate financial payback was to develop a new sales and marketing strategy for the relationship with their suppliers and for satisfying their customers' needs.

All of these case studies have one thing in common. They prove that it is important to devote resources at the initial planning stages of the market research to structure it carefully around the marketing problem. In this way the research will not only provide the information of interest to the company but also an indication as to which sales and marketing actions will be required. More importantly, it helps the company to think carefully about the payback from the investment in the market research through increased sales and marketing success.

## The action after the research

On completion of the research, the information provided should be used to help management understand:

- the market in which the company is operating, and the implications of such an environment.
- the attitudes and motivations of the company's present and potential customers and their criteria for selecting a company and its products or services in preference to competition.
- when new products and services are required and how to design them to meet the changing needs of existing and new customers.
- how to use the selection criteria and attitudes of the customers to develop communication and promotional themes so that their needs are satisfied; the end result of this being to persuade them to buy the company's product rather than those of competitors.

## Conclusion

It is seldom that the completion of a market research programme does not provide the basis for action. All market research can be cost-effective if it is designed to address the marketing and sales issues concerned. In order to do this, the company must:

- define carefully its marketing and sales strategy.
- agree the hypotheses or ideas that need to be proved or disproved to allow for the development of its strategy.
- research the total market and the mechanisms of that market rather than just the product or communications issues related to the market.
- decide on the likely actions it could take after the research, to assess them through the research adopted or identify what other actions are more essential.
- be prepared to use the findings of the research to improve the ways in which the company's total sales and marketing activities are run and how they relate to customer buying behaviour.

Research is necessary to ensure the effectiveness of marketing and thus it is not only a service to the marketing function, it is a means of directing the company to a successful future. A company has to accept that research:

- is only of use if it is acted on; it is both ineffective and costly if used for information purposes only.
- can provide a combination of information about the market, the strengths and weaknesses of its marketing methods and how they relate to the needs of its customers.
- must monitor the size, shape and nature of its markets; the needs of its markets; the opportunities and threats within the market; the marketing required to meet them; and the market gaps that exist and which present key areas of interest for the marketing strategies of the future to be focused on and pursued.

It is important to know the 'state of health' of the market and the performance of the company in the market, to the extent of measuring the success of individual sales and marketing methods. Without this knowledge a company cannot be sure of success and of taking the right decisions.

**140**

The action after the research is to use the research not only to take the right decisions, but to decide on actions that are realistic in relation to the product or service being marketed and the customer purchasing or using them. Research provides a company with the key to success when it is not merely solving a marketing problem, but has been carefully designed to provide direction and guidance for taking the right sales and marketing decisions.

**Checklist of questions for the effective use of market research**

- What decisions can I take?
- Which marketing consultancy company's experience will complement our requirements to help to take these decisions? – Does the company have experience in our specific market? – Do its executives understand not only the marketing problem, but ultimately what decisions we are likely to be faced with?
- How valid are the research results? – Are the desk research data derived from a reliable source? – Are the attitudes and opinions of the target sample sufficiently representative? – Does the questionnaire assess the market, as well as the needs of buyers and non-buyers, looking to prove or disprove the acceptance of new ideas or products in the marketplace?
- How can the research explore all elements of the market and the marketing problem?
- Will the research brief only provide information or will it also provide direction on our marketing and sales decisions?
- What evaluation needs to be carried out to identify: the effects of competitors' products and services? which market segments are not satisfied by the company? the behaviour of non-buyers or non-users? the traditional, current and future uses of the products or services? the benefits of the product or service?
- What are the required actions after the research?
- Do we know sufficiently well the market we are operating in and the implications of this environment for our company?
- What are the attitudes and motivations of the company's present and potential customers and their criteria for selecting our company and its products or services in preference to those of our competitors?

- Do we know when new products and services are required and how to design them to meet the changing needs of the customers and potential customers?
- How do we use the selection criteria and attitudes of the customers to develop communication and promotional themes so that their motivations are satisfied?
- How do we ensure that the company is taking all its decisions in the way that our customers think?
- Will the research we have designed produce the desired actions after the research? – Have we defined our marketing and sales strategy carefully? – Have we agreed the hypotheses or ideas that need to be proved or disproved to allow for the development of the strategy? – Does the research cover the total market and the mechanisms of that market rather than just the product or communications issues related to that market? – Have we decided on the likely actions that we could take after the research, to assess them through the research adopted or identify through the research what other actions are more essential? – Are we prepared to use the findings of the research to improve the ways in which our total sales and marketing activities are run and how they relate to the way in which our customers buy the products or services?
- Are we prepared to act on the research?
- Are we sure that the research is not for information purposes only and that it is both effective and cost-effective?
- Can the research provide a combination of information about the market, the strengths and weaknesses of our marketing methods, and how they relate to the needs of our customers?
- Is it monitoring the size, shape and nature of our markets, the needs of our markets, the opportunities and threats within our market, the marketing required to meet them, the market opportunities, the market gaps that exist and which present key areas of interest for the marketing strategies of the future to be focused on and pursued?
- Can we see 'life after the death of the research'?

# References and Recommended Reading List

The references used in the preparation of this book have been numerous to ensure that all possible ideas and traditional accounts of research have been taken into consideration. In addition, I have felt it important to make recommendations for the reader to refer to other publications to learn more about the techniques of research.

The most comprehensive reading list is published by the Education Committee of the Market Research Society. Publications referred to for the preparation of this book have included the following:

Worcester, R (1983) *Political Opinion Polling* Macmillan.

Worcester, R M and Downham, J (1986) *Consumer Market Research Handbook* 3rd edition. Van Nostrand Reinhold.

Green, P and Tull, J (1978) *Research for Marketing Decisions* 4th edition. Prentice Hall.

Crimp, M (1981) *The Marketing Research Process* Prentice Hall.

Bradley, U B (1987) *Applied Marketing and Social Research* Wiley.

Foxall, G R (1984) *Corporate Innovation: Marketing and Strategy* Croom Helm.

Oostveen, Jan C J (1986), *The State of Marketing Research in Europe* ESOMAR.

Lidstone, J (1978) *Motivating Your Sales Force* Gower Publishing.

Wilson, M T (1980) *The Management of Marketing* Gower Publishing.

Jain, A K, Pinson, P and Ratchford, B (1982) *Marketing Research - Applications and Problems* Wiley.

**143**

Majaro, S (1977) *International Marketing* George Allen & Unwin.

Hague, P N (1987) *The Industrial Market Research Handbook* Kogan Page.

Sowrey, P (1987) *The Generation of Ideas for New Products* Kogan Page.

Hague, P N and Jackson, P (1987) *Do Your Own Market Research* Kogan Page.

Case study material was also supplied by Richard Murray of Marketing Improvements Limited and includes information from an article by him which first appeared in *Management Today*. John Whitehead of CACI provided the ACORN data and Erhard Meir of RSL provided the SAGACITY information.

# Glossary of Terms

Market research is full of jargon and specific terminology for various techniques. A number of these have been referred to throughout the book. These terms are now listed below in more detail.

A full list of all the technical terms used in market research can be obtained by looking at the *Dictionary of Market Research* compiled by P A Talmage, published jointly by the Market Research Society Ltd (01-439 2585) and the Incorporated Society of British Advertisers Ltd (01-499 7502).

*advertising research* Any research into advertising except media research, particularly creative research, pre-tests of advertisements, and evaluation of advertising campaigns.

*advertising test* Research into the effectivenss of individual advertisements or of advertising campaigns. For pre-testing of individual advertisements, small-scale communication tests are often used. These employ techniques such as group discussions and hall tests, and, for print advertisements, folder tests. Post-testing may be based on recall methods, or on measuring behaviour and/or attitudes. Pre-/post-tests and tracking studies arc uscd for advertising campaign evaluation.

*brand image* The set of associations which a brand has acquired for an individual. In measuring brand images, the first step is to compile a list of the attributes of the brands in a market. Exploratory methods may be used for this purpose. The list may then be shortened to remove similar items. The ensuing quantitative stage may employ either rating scales, or sorting techniques such as the ascription of adjectives.

*brand positioning* The position of brands on a map, usually in two dimensions, which represent important factors influencing choice. These factors may include, eg, price, product attributes, user characteristics, and brand images.

*consumer research* Market research amongst consumers, as opposed to trade research and industrial market research.

*corporate image* The image of an enterprise as a whole, rather than of the particular goods or services which it supplies; the net result of interaction of all experiences, impressions, beliefs, feelings, and knowledge people have about the enterprise. Corporate image research often involves interviewing a number of groups or types of people, differing in the character of the interest that each has in the enterprise. Examples include shareholders, the City, employees and potential employees, customers, communities in which the enterprise has a presence, politicians, journalists and other 'opinion leaders'.

*corporate plan* A statement of a company's long-term objectives and how they are to be achieved.

*creative research* Research applied usually to the creation of advertisements. It embraces advertising pre-tests, communication tests, concept tests, copy tests, etc.

*customer research* Research amongst customers for a product or service.

*demographics* Demography is the study of births and deaths and of the ways in which these are affected by people's characteristics, background and social conditions. Demographic variables, eg sex, age, marital status and social grade, normally comprise a large part of the classification data obtained in market research interviews.

*depth interview* An informal face-to-face interview, which is only loosely structured, and appears more as a conversation than as a question-and-answer session. There are few direct questions. Respondents are instead encouraged to talk freely about the subject area, and the interviewer may probe to explore motivations, attitudes, etc.

*desk research* As opposed to the collection of primary data via field research, desk research is based on the use of secondary data, eg directories, lists, statistics, reports of past surveys and published information generally.

*distribution check* An observational survey of a sample of retail outlets, which measures the presence or otherwise of specified products, brands

**146**

and pack sizes. Prices and display may also be recorded.

*diversification study* Research to aid decisions concerning a possible diversification into some economic activity which is new to an enterprise.

*editorial research* Research to investigate the editorial content of newspapers, magazines and other media as products in their own right, rather than as vehicles for advertising.

*exploratory research* Research undertaken where little is already known about the subject, often as a preliminary to a survey. Relatively quick and cheap methods are usually employed -eg- desk research, group discussions, omnibus surveys and street or telephone interviews on a small scale.

*face-to-face interview* This fully descriptive term is to be preferred to the term personal interview, which may sometimes be taken to include both face-to-face and telephone interviews.

*family life cycle* Stages in the development of families, eg:

1. Bachelor stage – young single people living independently.
2. Young couples – no children.
3. Full nest – couples with children.
4. Empty nest – older couples, no children living with them.
5. Solitary survivors.

Group 3 is usually subdivided according to the age of the youngest child. Groups 4 and 5 may be subdivided according to whether the head of the household is still working or retired.

*field research* As opposed to desk research, the collection of primary data from external sources by means of surveys, observation and experiment.

*folder test* A method of pre-testing press advertisements, in which respondents are invited to look through a folder containing the test advertisements together with a number of control advertisements. Afterwards a number of questions are asked to establish what can be remembered, and to evaluate how effectively the test advertisement has imparted its message.

*group discussion* One of the basic methods of qualitative research, often used in exploratory work and when the subject matter involves social activities, habits and status. Used appropriately, group discussions elicit a large number of ideas in a short time, possibly including some that would not arise from individual interviews. They may be held in private houses or hired rooms, and typically last between one and two hours. Usually between six and twelve people are invited to participate. They are selected because they belong to the target group for the product or service under investigation, or are otherwise of interest to the study.

*hall test* A test for which people are taken to some fixed location, often a public hall or pub. This is commonly done for advertisement, pack and product tests, where the equipment or supplies required cannot conveniently be taken into private homes or carried around the streets, and for tests which need controlled conditions.

*image* People's perceptions or impressions of a product, service, company, person, etc, however these may have been formed, and however much they reflect reality. Image research sets out to discover perceived strengths and weaknesses, relative to the images of competitors or of an ideal, which may then be exploited or repaired as appropriate.

*industrial market research* Defined by the Industrial Marketing Research Association as the systematic, objective and exhaustive search for and study of facts relevant to any problem in the field of industrial marketing.

*industrial marketing* All business and activities involving or influencing the movement of industrial products from the manufacturer to the industrial or commercial user.

*industrial products* Materials, machinery and capital equipment used by and services provided for industrial and institutional establishments.

*in-house research* Research conducted by the organization that wants the information, rather than by a research agency, etc, acting on its behalf.

*interview* A contact with an informant, or sometimes a group of informants, in order to obtain information for a research project. This generally involves an interviewer or some other representative of the organization carrying out the project, whether actually present or by means of the telephone. The term is not usually applied to such activities as the completion of diaries or postal questionnaires, or observations of behaviour.

*mapping* Rules or formulae by which the elements in one set can each be made to correspond to a single element in a second set. Any sort of diagrammatic or symbolic representation.

*market intelligence* Information about current events in the outside world, that may be of use in market planning.

*market map* A diagram which shows the relative positions of brands in terms of the most important brand characteristics, sometimes used to summarize the findings of attitude research. In its simplest form it presents just two characteristics as a pair, eg high price/low price and high quality/low quality, and each brand is represented by a point between these two.

*market planning* The preparation of marketing plans and forecasts for operation use within the organization, including the collation and analysis of all relevant information, and the assessment of sales and marketing performance.

*market positioning* How a product or brand relates to its competitors in terms of, eg, product attributes, price, channels of sale, product usage, consumer characteristics.

*market research* Market research has sometimes been distinguished from marketing research, to mean the collection of data about markets by means of surveys. Either term is more usually taken to comprise both the systematic collection from external sources of any information about markets, and the analysis of this information for market planning and business decisions generally. Analyses for marketing purposes of internal data such as sales statistics and customer records are sometimes included, but not information which arises directly from accounting procedures, operational research and similar distinct spheres of professional competence. Information about events in the outside world is counted as market research only when obtained in the course of a survey; otherwise this falls under the heading of market intelligence.

*market share* The proportion of a market accounted for by a particular brand or supplier, either by volume or by value or sometimes in terms of the number of consumers. It depends in practice on a precise definition of what constitutes the market, at what point it is to be measured (wholesale or retail value, manufacturers' deliveries or consumers' purchases, etc) and how completely it is covered by the chosen method of measurement, and the period to which the measurement relates.

*marketing* Defined by the Institute of Marketing as the management function responsible for identifying, anticipating and satisfying consumer requirements profitably. The term is commonly used in at least three senses: as a concept or philosophy of business, as one function of management alongside finance, personnel, etc, and to denote a set of related business techniques.

*marketing audit* An inventory of information relevant to the marketing of a product or service.

*marketing control* A set of marketing objectives together with measurements which show the extent to which these objectives are met.

*marketing information system* The whole of the information, from whatever source, which is available to marketing management, together with its storage, processing and retrieval. Market research is a part of this system, as also are market intelligence and reports from accounting and other internal sources.

*marketing mix* The set of choices made by an organization in respect of those market factors which it can control. Important categories in the marketing mix are the so-called four Ps, namely product, price, place and promotion. Each of these may be regarded as a heading under which individual elements may be grouped, eg the first covers brand name, packaging, sizes, varieties, etc, as well as the attributes of the product as such.

*marketing services* All activities, other than actual selling, that assist marketing activities.

*motivation research* Small-scale studies aimed at discovering reasons for people's behaviour.

*name test* Any investigation into the effectiveness of a proposed name, or a short-list of candidate names, often as part of a programme of research for a new product. It may cover, eg, how easily a name can be pronounced, its on-pack visibility, its memorability and associations, and what people infer about the qualities of the product.

*observation* The alternative to questioning as a way of obtaining primary data. It includes any kind of measurement and any means of perception, ie not only visual observation.

*operational research* The application of a variety of mathematical and statistical techniques to rationalizing operations and improving efficiency, in areas of business activity such as industry, commerce, administration, production and engineering.

*opinion poll* A survey of opinions about political, social and other issues of public interest, especially as a basis for forecasting voting behaviour. Opinion polls are often commissioned by the media for editorial purposes, or are published in the hope of promoting the interests of a political party or pressure group.

*point-of-sale research* Research into the effectiveness of point-of-sale material. Any survey conducted at the point of sale, ie surveys amongst samples of customers or people emerging from a shop.

*poster research* Research to measure audiences for outdoor advertising.

*post-test* A test of advertising after it has been exposed to the public in the normal way. Despite the name given to it, such research may not be true experimentation. It is usually based on surveys measuring, eg, recall and recognition of the advertising, brand awareness and image.

*pricing research* Any kind of research which aims to show how demand for a product or service will vary with its price.

*product life cycle* The idea that products are analogous to living organisms, passing through stages which are usually identified as introduction, growth, maturity and decline.

*product test* Any research in which consumers, or potential customers, are invited to try out a product. It is not necessarily an experiement as such. There are many ways of carrying out product tests, depending on the nature of the product and the kind of information sought. The term is not used to describe opinion surveys concerning products which consumers have bought in the normal way, whether or not during a test market.

*profile* A description of a group of people, in terms of their sex, age, and other demographics, and possibly their behaviour and attitudes.

*promotional research* Any kind of market research concerned with consumer or trade promotions.

*qualitative* 1. Relating to an attribute, eg sex, rather than to a quantitative variable. 2. Relating to qualitative research.

*qualitative research* A body of research techniques which can primarily be distinguished from quantitative methods because they do not attempt to make measurements. Instead, they seek insights through a less structured, more flexible approach. Often they try to explore motivations, hence the earlier term motivational research. Typical methods are group discussions and depth interviews, which, like all qualitative research, are based on small samples.

*questionnaire* A list of questions, sometimes termed a question schedule, an interview schedule, or a recording schedule. A questionnaire is usually printed, but may appear on a computer screen, as in computer-assisted telephone interviewing or occasionally in hall tests, etc. It normally includes instructions as to its use, and provides for the recording of answers and administrative details, as well as showing the actual questions.

*rating scale* A scale used by a respondent when answering a question. The term is not usually employed unless the respondent has at least three choices. The actual scale may be verbal, eg agree/disagree scale, diagrammatic, or numerical.

*readership research* Surveys which aim to estimate the numbers and characteristics of people who read a newspaper or magazine, as distinct from the numbers who buy it.

*retail audit* A method of obtaining information about the movement of consumer products into and out of retail outlets. It uses a panel which is constituted by a representative sample of outlets of a particular type, or of several types where products are distributed through a variety of outlets. Audits are carried out at regular intervals such as every four weeks or two months.

*sample* A part or subset of a population. Its purpose is to enable investigation of the characteristics of the population at reduced cost in terms of time, effort and money. A sample must therefore be representative of the whole.

*sample size* The number of units in a sample, eg the number of individuals in a sample of people, or the number of households in a sample of households, or the number of purchasing occasions in a sample of purchasing occasions. Larger sample sizes produce estimates of greater precision.

*sampling* The process of selecting a sample. In the organization of a survey, however, the sampling stage is generally regarded as preceding fieldwork, so that any element of field sampling becomes a part of the latter stage.

*secondary data* As distinguished from primary data collected for the specific purpose in hand, secondary data are those which have been collected for some other reason. The main sources of secondary data are: internal records maintained for operating, accounting and other administrative purposes; government statistical and other publications; books and periodicals, especially directories and trade magazines; commercial information services and syndicated surveys. Others include reports of past research, company financial statements and trade associations.

*segmentation* Division of a market into parts, each of which has identifiable characteristics of actual or potential economic interest. Most often segmentation is in terms either of characteristics of the product or service, or of purchaser/user characteristics. Sometimes methods of sales and distribution form a viable basis. Performance, specialized applications, other product attributes, and price are used for product-based segmentation. Segmentations of consumer markets based on purchaser/user characteristics include: reasons for purchase, eg gifts/own use/family use; mode of usage and other product-related behavioural characteristics; purchase criteria and attitudes towards the product; geographic, demographic and psychographic classifications. Industrial markets are often segmented by customer size and industrial classification.

*social class* 1. A synonym for socio-economic class. 2. A classification used in the Census of Population which depends on present or former occupation:

I       Professional etc
II      Intermediate
III(N)  Skilled non-manual
III(M)  Skilled manual
IV      Partly skilled
IV      Armed forces and inadequately described occupations.
V       Unskilled.

*social grade* The socio-economic classification system used by the National Readership Survey, and generally for market research in the UK. The social grade of an informant is based on the occupation or former occupation of the head of the family unit, or in certain circumstances, eg where the head of the family unit is retired or unemployed and has a low income, it may be based on the occupation of the chief wage earner. Usually this person is also the head of household. If such information cannot be obtained, the assessment is based on environmental factors such as the type of dwelling, amenities, the presence of domestic help, etc. The classes are as shown on p 140.

| Grade | Social Status | Occupation |
|---|---|---|
| A | **Upper middle class** | Higher managerial/administrative/professional |
| B | **Middle class** | Intermediate managerial/administrative/professional |
| C1 | **Lower middle class** | Supervisory or clerical and junior managerial/administrative/professional |
| C2 | **Skilled working class** | Skilled manual workers |
| D | **Working class** | Semi- and unskilled manual workers |
| E | **Those at lowest levels of subsistence** | State pensioners or widows (no other earnings), casual or lowest grade workers |

The six classes are often combined into four (AB/C1/C2/DE) or into two (ABC1/C2DE).

*strategic plan* A statement of long-term objectives for a business or brand, how in broad terms these objectives are to be achieved, and how resources are to be allocated for the purpose.

*survey* The systematic collection, analysis and interpretation of information about some subject of study. In market research, the term is particularly used to signify the collection of information by means of sampling and interviews with the selected individuals or with proprietors or employees for samples of businesses, etc. Desk research projects and observational studies may also be described as surveys.

*test market* The launch of a new product or service in a limited area or areas, enacting on a small scale a planned introductory programme. The main purpose is usually to forecast the results of a wider-scale launch. It may also serve to uncover deficiencies in the marketing plan or its execution, which can be remedied for a subsequent national launch; this function is termed pilot marketing. Research techniques used to monitor test markets include particularly retain audits and distribution checks, consumer panels and tracking studies.

# Useful Addresses

## Government departments

*United Kingdom*

**British Overseas Trade Board**
Export Marketing Research Section
1 Victoria Street
London SW1H 0ET
01-215 5277 (Firms A–I)
01-215 5285 (Firms J–Z)
Regional offices in Belfast, Bristol, Birmingham, Cardiff, Glasgow, Leeds, London, Manchester, Newcastle upon Tyne and Nottingham

**Business Statistics Office**
Cardiff Road
Newport
Gwent NPT 1XG
0633 56111

**Central Office of Information**
Hercules Road
London SE1 7DU
01-928 2345

**Central Statistical Office**
Great George Street
London SW1P 3AQ
01-233 6135/6193

**Companies House**
112 City Road
London EC1Y 1AY
01-253 9393

**Companies Registration Office**
102 George Street
Edinburgh EH2 3DJ
031-225 5774

**Department of Employment**
Caxton House
Tothill Street
London SW1H 9NF
01-213 3000

**Department of Energy**
Thames House South
Millbank
London SW1P 4QJ
01-211 3000

**Departments of the Environment and Transport**
2 Marsham Street
London SW1P 3EB
01-212 3434

**Government Actuary's Department**
22 Kingsway
London WC2B 6JP
01-242 6828

**HM Customs and Excise**
Bill of Entry Service, Statistical Office
Portcullis House
27 Victoria Avenue
Southend-on-Sea SS2 6AL
0702 49421

**HMSO Books**
PO Box 569
London SE1 9NH
01-928 1321

**Ministry of Agriculture, Fisheries and Food**
Whitehall Place
London SW1A 2HH
01-233 5550

**Ministry of Defence**
5 Northumberland House
London WC2N 5BP
01-218 9000

**National Economic Development Office**
Millbank Tower
Millbank
London SW1P 4QX
01-211 6886

**Office of Population Censuses and Surveys**
St Catherine's House
Kingsway
London WC2B 6JP
01-242 0262

**Registrar of Companies**
Companies House
Crown Way
Maindy
Cardiff CF4 3UZ
0222 388588

**Statistics and Market Intelligence Library**
1 Victoria Street
London SW1H 0ET
01-215 5444

*United States of America*
**Anti-Trust Division of Department of Justice**
10th Stand Constitution Avenue NW
Washington
DC 20530
General Information: (202) 633 2683
Librarian: (202) 633 2431

**157**

**Bureau of the Census**
Data Users Services Division
Statistical Compendia Staff
Washington
DC 20233
(301) 763 5299

**Census Office of Public Affairs**
US Department of Commerce
Federal Office Building No 3
Room 2705
Washington
DC 20233
(301) 763 4051

**Minority Business Development Agency**
US Department of Commerce
Room H5063
Washington
DC 20230
(202) 377 1936

**Office of the Director**
National Technical Information Service
5285 Port Royal Road
Springfield
VA 22161
(703) 487 4636

**US Government Printing Office**
Washington
DC 20402
(202) 783 3238

**Publishers**
*United Kingdom*
**Aslib**
27 Boswell Street
London WC1N 3JZ
01-430 2671

**Business Surveys Ltd**
(Research Index)
PO Box 21
Dorking
Surrey RH5 4EE
0306 887857

**CBD Research Limited**
*(Directory of European Associations; Directory of Directories; Statistics Europe)*
154 High Street
Beckenham
Kent BR3 1EA
01-650 7745

**Dun & Bradstreet**
(Publications Division for *Key British Enterprises, Who Owns Whom*)
6–8 Bonhill Street
London EC2A 4BU
01-377 4377

**Extel Financial Ltd**
37–45 Paul Street
London EC2A 4PB
01-253 3400

**Inter Company Comparisons Ltd**
28–42 Banner Street
London EC1Y 8QE
01-253 3906

**IPC Business Press Information Services Ltd**
(Kelly's Directories etc)
Windsor Court
East Grinstead House
East Grinstead
West Sussex RH19 1XA
0342 26972

**Kompass Publishers Ltd**
Windsor Court
East Grinstead House

**159**

East Grinstead
West Sussex RH19 1XA
0342 26972

**McCarthy Information Ltd**
Manor House
Ash Walk
Warminster
Wiltshire BA12 8PY
0986 215151

**Predicasts International Incorporated**
(for Predicasts; World Regional Casts; Prompt)
199–201 High Street
Orpington
Kent BR6 0PF
0689 38488

*United States of America*

**Business Research Publications**
817 Broadway
New York
NY 10003
(212) 673 4700
(MacRae's *Blue Book*)

**Business Yellow Pages**
MPO Box 2008
Niagara Falls
NY 14302

**Dun & Bradstreet International**
1 World Trade Centre
Suite 9069
New York
NY 10048
(212) 938 8400

**Gale Research Company**
Book Tower

Detroit
Michigan 48226
(Statistical Sources; Directory of Special Libraries and Information
Centre; Encyclopedia of Business Information Sources; Encyclopedia
of Associations; Trade Names Dictionary)

**Moody's Investors Series**
99 Church Street
New York
NY 10007
(212) 553 0300

**National Register Publishing Company**
3004 Glenview Road
Wilmette
Illinois 60091
(312) 256 6067
(*Director of Corporate Affiliations*)

**Standard & Poor's Corporation**
25 Broadway
New York
NY 10004
(212) 208 8702

**Thomas Publishing Company**
One Penn Plaza
New York
NY 10001
(212) 695 0500
(*Thomas's Register*)

**International organizations**

**Commission of the European Communities Press &
Information Office**
8 Storey's Gate
London SW1P 3AT
01-222 8122

**Commission of the European Communities**
200 rue de la Loi
1049 Brussels
Belgium

**The Council of Europe**
Avenue de l'Europe
67006 Strasbourg
France

**European Free Trade Association (EFTA)**
9–11 rue de Varembe
CH–1211 Geneva 20
Switzerland

**Food & Agriculture Organization (FAO)**
Via delle Terme di Caracalla
00100 Rome
Italy

**General Agreement on Tariffs and Trade (GATT)**
Centre William Rappard
154 rue de Lausanne
CH–1211 Geneva 21
Switzerland

**International Bank for Reconstruction and Development
(IBRD – World Bank)**
1818 H Street NW
Washington
DC20433
USA

**International Labour organization (ILO)**
CH–1211 Geneva 22
Switzerland

**International Monetary Fund (IMF)**
700 19th Street NW
Washington
DC 20431
USA

**United States Conference on Trade & Development (UNCTAD)**
Palais des Nations
CH–1211 Geneva 10
Switzerland

**United Nations Economic Commission for Europe**
Palais des Nations
CH–12111 Geneva 10
Switzerland

**United Nations Educational, Scientific & Cultural Organizations (UNESCO)**
7 Place de Fontenoy
75707 Paris
France

**United Nations Industrial Development Organization (UNIDO)**
PO Box 300
1400 Vienna
Austria

**United Nations Information Centre**
Ship House
20 Buckingham Gate
London SW1E 6LB

**World Health Organization (WHO)**
Avenue Appia
CH–1211 Geneva 27
Switzerland

# Index

# Index

# Index

# UNRULY WOMEN